Faith on the Mountain

Front cover: Photograph of a quilt made by Barbara Louv.
The original quilt hangs on a wall in the Bonny Doon Church.

Faith on the Mountain

Spiritual Stories
from the Bonny Doon Church

By

Members of Bonny Doon Presbyterian Church

Edited by

Barbara Gaskell and Helen Gibbons

Contents

Editors' Note

We would like to thank every Bonny Doon Church member who contributed to this book. It has been a joy for us to work with each one of you. Your stories fascinated us, inspired us, and brought us closer to God.

Preface

Here at the Bonny Doon Church we are united by our faith in Jesus Christ, and by our commitment to love and cherish one another. The Bible describes the church as being like a human body. We are *one* body. We need each other; we cannot be complete without each other, and each of us has special gifts to offer the others. But as individuals we are as different as the hills. Just as an eye is nothing like an ear, and a hand is nothing like a tongue, even though they are all part of one body, we are each utterly unique. So it is with our stories. God meets us where we are, in each of our different places, and gently and patiently draws us toward faith in Him and in our Lord Jesus Christ. There are no cookie-cutter Christians.

We are writing down these stories for the encouragement of one another, and for the encouragement of you, our reader, whoever you may be. Our God is an amazing and wonderful God, and we rejoice in what He has done in each of our lives. Each story of God's hand at work in a human life is precious. These are some of ours.

The church is not a gallery for the exhibition of eminent Christians, but a school for the education of imperfect ones, a nursery for the care of weak ones, a hospital for the healing of those who need assiduous care.

Henry Ward Beecher[1]

This quote was on the church bulletin every Sunday for many years and was appreciated by many of us.

---

1 From *A Dictionary of Thoughts: Being a Cyclopedia of Laconic Quotations* by Tryon Edwards, published by F.B. Dickerson Company, 1908, page 73.

Finding Love

Dane Hardin

When I was growing up, my only consistent exposure to matters of faith was when my parents said prayers with my sister and me after we were in bed for the night—simple prayers, like "Now I lay me down to sleep. . . ." One time when my Dad was sitting on the edge of my bed at prayer time, he said, "You know, Jesus was the only perfect man." As far as I can remember, those were the only words of faith I ever heard from my father.

I was a trying child, especially for my mother. When we were in department stores and she said, "Don't touch the things on the shelf," I touched the things on the shelf. On the Myers-Briggs personality type indicator, I have a very high S, indicating I am sensate. I have to experience things by every means possible and I HAD to touch the things on the shelf. I remember times when my mother would say to me in absolute frustration, "Dane, what is *wrong* with you?" Those words went to my soul, as I will explain later.

When I was growing up, church meant for me that I had to put on tight, uncomfortable clothes and go to a place where I would hear not very understandable and severe messages from a severe person. This was not an experience that gave me life, and I did not like church. I could also see from my Dad's upbringing that, at least in his life, Christianity was the religion of "No." You couldn't do any fun things if you were a Christian. My Dad did manage to do forbidden fun things, just not when my grandfather was around. I never learned that God could be a loving, forgiving, living presence in people's lives. I had no concept of that. In fact, God became the person that I held responsible for all the bad things that happened to me, and there were occasions when I actually cursed at God.

As I grew up, and at a pretty early age, I realized that I had the gift, or maybe it was the burden, of making people laugh. To this day Kathy cringes when my one-liners come out in church. It is like she is saying, "Okay, there you go, again. You've spoken without thinking." And she is absolutely right. But, for comedians, timing is everything. So if I miss the moment, the humor is gone, and I find it irresistible to seize that moment and make myself the center of attention.

I also gained the knack for knowing everything, having the last word in any argument. I was the person who knew it all, and I made people laugh. These were the attributes I developed to help me get through my childhood—to be accepted. I was the 90-pound weakling that I read about in Charles Atlas bodybuilding ads on matchbooks. These ads showed the 90-pound weakling having sand kicked in his face by the bodybuilder on the beach. I did everything I could not to appear that way. In high school, I was mostly on cruise control, but I remember practicing looking cool. And I still present that practiced look of nonchalance.

I came to UC Santa Cruz as a junior transfer student in the first year the school opened, 1965. After two years, I graduated. It was the summer after I graduated in 1967 that I was introduced to marijuana. The euphoria and the sense of well being it gave me made me think that as long as I had marijuana, my life was going to be beautiful. It gave me hope for the future.

Kathy and I began dating in the fall of 1967. She had also come to UCSC in 1965, but as a freshperson. In 1967, she went to the Urbana Student Missions Conference, sponsored by InterVarsity Christian Fellowship, with a group of Christian students from University Baptist Church.[2] While she was there, she gave her life to Christ during the large, 40- to 60-thousand student worship service. This had quite an impact on her. She forgave her father for the pain he caused her family. But I was not interested in what she had to say. I was too busy having fun, and I felt absolutely no need for what Kathy said she had received by giving her life to Jesus.

So there we were, Kathy—as much as she could be—devoted to Jesus, and I—as much as I could be—devoted to marijuana. And we got married. I know that seems crazy, but we were young and looking for love in all the wrong places. We made the decision to marry for completely broken reasons. And pretty quickly, Kathy went on antidepressants. It was like she said to herself, "Oh my goodness, what have I done?" At that time, she was a graduate student at Cal State Hayward, getting her master's in math. So for at least one of us, this match (that we could later say was made in heaven) was having a huge negative effect.

For the first year or two of our marriage, I attended University Baptist Church with Kathy, and I was pretty astonished by what I saw there. I experienced people who loved me and accepted me just as I was. They were not put off by my long hair and attire. (I think maybe I originated the "grunge" look that eventually Seattle adopted.) There I was with my Levis, flannel shirt, and work boots, and they loved me. But I eventually drifted away because I felt no need for what church could offer. I lacked belief. There was nothing there that really gripped my soul or my spirit, and the idea of a personal relationship with something I couldn't see was just plain weird to me. Marvin Webster was the pastor at that time, and when we

---

2 Now renamed High Street Community Church.

had dinner at his house he would talk to me about faith. He would say, "Where do you get your spiritual filling?" And I would answer, "In the woods. I really connect with nature." So, he would ask, "Well, can you have a personal relationship with nature?" But the question didn't budge me—I felt like I did have a personal relationship with nature, but I didn't want to hear about Jesus.

There came a point when Kathy and I were going to go our separate ways. Actually, I was going to go *my* separate way, and I had a date set. I was going to move in with my supervisor at work. Marvin Webster found out about this. He had seen Kathy at church and she was pretty distraught, so he asked her what was going on. She told him that I was going to be leaving. A few days later he knocked on our front door and asked if we could talk. I said, "Sure." He wanted to know if I was willing to see a marriage and family therapist (a Christian woman named Donna Wilder) if he paid for the first three visits. We had already seen a counselor through the university, and that person had hoped that she could get Kathy to agree that we should separate. I agreed to Marvin's offer. I cared for Kathy, and Kathy cared for me, and after seeing Donna for the three visits paid for by Marvin, she was convinced that she could help us save our marriage. We stuck with it, and through Donna's love and wisdom, we grew in our ability to communicate and work together on our relationship. We eventually had kids, and Kathy and I have been blessed by our life together since then.

But through all those early years of marriage, having kids and building a house in Bonny Doon, I maintained a pretty constant relationship with marijuana. I had myself convinced that there was nothing wrong with it—after all, it only affected me. Kathy and the girls would get dressed up and go off to church on

Sunday, and I would go out in the woods and smoke a joint. One Sunday morning when our older daughter was about four or five, and she was all dressed up in her beautiful frilly Sunday dress, she said, "Daddy, don't you want to come to church with us and learn about God?" It gives me chills to think about that moment. It had a big impact on me. While I felt it deeply, I was not ready to change. I was not ready to give up the things that I was hanging on to. There came a time not long after this, when I began getting stomach aches whenever Kathy and the girls were getting ready for church. I knew enough about myself to know that my anxiety settles in my intestines. That is where I feel it. That anxiety was coming from internal conflict over my use of marijuana. But I still wasn't ready to change.

The first time I clearly heard God speak to me—although I didn't necessarily attribute it to God at the time—was one Sunday when I was getting ready to light a pipe of something while Kathy and the girls were at church, and these words came into my head: "If you really think there is nothing wrong with this, why are you hiding it?" Kathy had no clue that I was smoking while she was at church because I had been hiding it. I had no good answer for that question. I realized that it was time to give up smoking marijuana, or at least stop sneaking around.

Not long after that, on a Sunday morning when Kathy and the girls were in the kitchen ready to go to church, I showed up and said, "Can I come with you?" Kathy's jaw dropped, and I think, though I might be making this up, that she stammered, "Well, sure." She was flabbergasted. She had no clue that this was coming. At that point, I had become interested in exploring faith. I wanted to see what Christian life was all about, but I was not ready to make a commitment.

Around this time, University Baptist Church had an outreach event and invited Haddon Robinson to speak. He was a renowned teacher, preacher, and author who grew up in Hell's Kitchen in New York. Though not physically attractive, he was a compelling speaker. He laid out the "trilemma" popularized by C.S. Lewis as "Liar, Lunatic, or Lord."[3] The argument goes like this: When you look at Jesus and hear what he says about himself, you really have only three choices about what to think of him. Either he was a liar, who said he was the son of God and knew he wasn't. Or, he was a lunatic, who said that he was the son of God and *didn't know* he wasn't. Or he was who he said he was—the son of God. Haddon Robinson also told several stories of people who had set out to discredit Jesus' claims, but had been drawn to faith in Jesus as a result of their investigations. His words really made me think, and he left me with a lot to chew on.

At about the same time, Eldridge Cleaver, who was a member of the Black Panther Party, came to speak at the Santa Cruz Civic Auditorium. I was a strong supporter of the Black Panther Party in their heyday and believed in their battles for justice for the African American community. Cleaver had been in exile in Algeria, avoiding prosecution for crimes he had committed, and he came back professing faith in Jesus. He had a salvation experience in which he saw the face of Jesus in the full moon. Kathy and I went to see him, and, again, I was brought to an important inflection point in my faith journey. In his later years, I am afraid brother Eldridge went off the tracks, but what I heard him say that night was instrumental in getting me to open myself up to God. I was ready to learn who Jesus was and consider what He had to say in an objective way. At that point,

---

3 https://en.wikipedia.org/wiki/Lewis%27s_trilemma

my image of God began to morph from my childhood nemesis to the person I thanked for the good things in my life.

By then I was in my late 30's. I became involved in a project that had me working on a ship at sea for two or three weeks at a time. It was a fascinating project in which we were using a two-man submersible to collect data from the bottom of the ocean. When I left for one of the cruises, Kathy gave me a tiny version of the gospels. On the ship, I would lie in my bunk at night with the light over my head reading this tiny print that recounted Jesus' life on earth. And I remember realizing, as an echo of my father's only words about Christianity, that Jesus was perfect. If we all lived as He did, this world would be a perfect place. It was that realization that made me decide that He was a person I wanted to follow.

I also realized in reading the gospels that Jesus was not crazy, even though His family thought He was at times. Jesus was not deceitful; instead He was honest, at times brutally honest. He was a truth teller.

So I set my course to follow Jesus, but I didn't completely stop smoking marijuana. I didn't go looking for it, but in a quirk of self deceit, I reasoned that if it came to me, God must want me to smoke it. Yeah, I know that sounds pretty wacky. Then I came across Ephesians 5:18, where it says, "Do not get drunk on wine, which leads to debauchery. Instead, be filled with the Spirit." (New International Version) I had to acknowledge that I only smoked marijuana to get high, to escape from my mind. That verse from Ephesians was the encouragement I needed to change. As this was transpiring, my friends who smoked would look at me askance as they went off to get high, while I withdrew to be alone with nature, or to read my Bible.

Sometime around then, I had my second real encounter with the Holy Spirit. This encounter was completely mind-blowing. I was involved in another project in the Santa Barbara Channel and was down there with a crew of three other people. We were working on a large boat trying to recover instruments that we had put on the ocean bottom months before. We were using high-tech equipment to get it back. Some of the instruments were not responding to our signals and never popped to the surface. Another of the instruments we were trying to recover was lost as we attempted to bring it on deck. It was a long, discouraging day, with very little to show for our efforts.

When the day was finished, we loaded up our van, had dinner in Santa Barbara, and set off for Santa Cruz. I was driving and it was about 11:30 or 12:00 at night. Everyone else in the van was asleep. We were on Highway 1, near Moss Landing, when a car pulled in front of us from a side road. It was going the same direction we were going, and it was going very slowly, so I pulled up behind it. In the headlights I saw the back of the driver's head, and I realized that I knew the person. He was a very good friend of mine. His wife had been a trailer mate of Kathy's in her first year at UCSC. I thought, 'This is really strange.' He was headed back towards the Watsonville area, where they lived, and I was really puzzled about seeing him out so late along a dark stretch of Highway 1.

A few days later I called these friends and invited them to our house for dinner. As we were eating, I asked my friend, "Where were you last Thursday night?" In shock, he responded, "Huh, who have you been talking to?" His wife volunteered that he had gone out to commit suicide. He had driven to the beach, loaded the gun, but eventually decided not to go through with it.

And when I think about that encounter on a dark Highway 1, I think about my foot on the accelerator for the last 250 miles, and how long it took us to get the gear off the boat and eat dinner in Santa Barbara. If we had gotten to that point on Highway 1 in Moss Landing 10 seconds earlier, I would not have seen my friend. His wife told me, "Dane, the Holy Spirit is really on you," and I have no other explanation. The coincidence is nothing short of miraculous. Absolutely. I don't know if that chance encounter was for my benefit or for my friend's, but I know that subsequently at a marriage encounter, he acknowledged that he was under the protection of a higher power. So, my own personal experience showed me that the Holy Spirit is real and works in our lives in ways that we simply can't explain.

A few years later, I was working in Kazakhstan on oil-development projects doing environmental impact studies. There I connected with a group of American missionaries, and my heart was opened for the Kazakh people. I was just in love with them, and I felt God calling me there. I came back and shared this vision with Kathy, and she was nearly distraught. She had barely made it through the required four quarters of German she had to take in university. She can't hear the nuances of foreign sounds, and to contemplate having to learn a new language and be in a completely foreign place where she wouldn't know anyone was not a life-giving prospect for her.

I was puzzled by her response and very upset, and I kept pushing, which just made things worse for Kathy. I felt that I was doing this big thing for God—an important thing for God—and my wife wouldn't cooperate. What in the world was going on? One day I was sitting in my home office praying, and I was beseeching God, "What should I do about this?" I very clearly heard a voice say, "Love your wife."   The voice was not emphatic; it was matter-of-fact—"Love your wife"—and I *got* it immediately. I said, "Okay, then in your time, God." Not only did I know this word was from God and meant specifically for me, but it was affirming. It taught me a real truth about God, that God's economy is not what we think it is. It is more important to Him that we love the people around us, rather than leave them in the dust to go do something we think is really important, even if it is for God. Love was the big message.

Shortly after that I became involved in contemplative practices through Don Ferris, the pastor at High Street Community Church, and his wife Charlotte. This involved guided monthly spiritual retreats. We were given scriptures and questions, and we spent time in silence and solitude, inviting God into our souls.

On one of our monthly retreats, I was sitting in a quiet corner with my knees pulled up in front of me, my eyes closed, and my head resting on my knees. I was totally stressed at the time. I was over-committed, and I felt like I was going to fall apart. I was asking God, "Why am I so stressed?" His word eventually came to me very clearly. What I heard was, "Because you have a tender heart." This was affirming to me because it was an acknowledgment of a good characteristic in my soul and my way of being. But it also subsequently helped heal my soul, because it showed me one of the reasons why I took on too much. I was over-extended because I craved the sense of importance that came with fulfilling needs—even to the detriment of myself and those I loved. In this regard, I don't think I am that unusual frankly; I think there are many of us that could fit in this category. For me, at that time and place, this realization continued God's work in my life, bringing me to a deeper awareness of God as the lover of my soul.

On another of our monthly retreats, the topic was exploring how God views our sins. It was near the end of the day when suddenly an image came into my head. It was the image of the hen that Jesus described in Matthew 23:37, when he was lamenting over Jerusalem: ". . . How often I have longed to gather your children together, as a hen gathers her chicks under her wings. . . ." (NIV) God was showing me that while I was considering my own sin, Jesus was not pushing me away. He was drawing me closer. I have continued to see that again and again. When I foul up, when I backslide, Jesus is there to catch me. He is wanting me to come closer to Him. He is not condemning me or pushing me away.

Another experience I had with the Holy Spirit was in a very improbable place. One day I was driving to our company headquarters in Livermore. I was on Highway 280 between 17 and 680, and a voice came into my head. It said, "You know, you don't always have to be right." Immediately I thought, 'What! What are you talking about?' But as I contemplated these words, things started popping up. 'Oh yeah, with your co-workers—Oh yeah, with your wife—Oh yeah, you always have to have the last word. You have to know everything about everything, and you always have to be right. This is an ego thing for you.'

I know these voices that speak to my soul are not my own because if they had been mine, my inner critic would have been saying, 'You stupid jerk! Who do you think you are, that you always have to be right?' Instead, the voice I hear is what I call Thumper's mother's voice. In the movie *Bambi*, Thumper was a little rabbit. Do you remember what Thumper's mother would say? She had a very sweet, sincere, and musical voice.

She would say, "Thumper, Thumper, if you can't say anything nice, don't say anything at all." That is the voice I hear. It is not my voice. Every time I have heard this voice, it has told me revolutionary things. It has made me aware of things in my own life, has encouraged me to consider them, and has shown me how those attributes in my life affect other people. It has encouraged me to go to Jesus with them and work on the needs in my soul that have caused me to be that way.

I have learned that Jesus is a gracious and merciful God. You see this time and again in the scriptures; for example, in the story of Zacchaeus the tax collector (Luke 19). Zacchaeus was reviled by the Israelites because he was a collaborator with the occupying Roman government, collecting their taxes. He wanted to see Jesus, but he was short, so he climbed a tree. Jesus saw him up in the tree and said to him, "Zacchaeus, come down immediately. I must stay at your house today." (NIV) Jesus was saying, "I want to be with you, Zacchaeus!" Wow! As another example, I think about the woman caught in adultery (John 8). Jesus didn't condemn her. In fact, His response was to ask all the people who were condemning her, "Do you have sin in your own lives? Let those of you without sin be the first to cast a stone at her." They were going to kill her and Jesus forgave her.

My experiences of seeking Jesus and inviting His presence into my soul, and the experiences of receiving His love in the deepest recesses of my being, have changed me. Through His touch, I am less imprisoned by the practiced, self-created, and unconscious ways of being that I built to protect myself from shame and humiliation in my childhood. And I am not unique in that way. We all have deep wounds that we have calloused over. We all have ways of being that have protected us and kept us from being the real persons that Jesus created us to be.

   This process of transformation through the love of Christ has shown me that the Christian faith is a journey and not a destination. I am blessed to be a lifelong learner. I still keep hearing things; in fact, it was just in the last two months that I woke up in the morning hearing my mother say, "Dane, what is *wrong* with you?" But then I was able to connect this with an incident that occurred when I was in junior college. I was sitting in the front seat of my car with my girlfriend of the time, and I collapsed into tears. I don't remember what we were talking about, but I was sobbing on her shoulder, "What is wrong with me? What is wrong with me?" I didn't know what was wrong with me, I just knew that I felt really broken in my innermost being. At the time, I didn't connect this with what my mother had told me years before. I didn't realize that I had absorbed my mother's words inside myself. So this is a lifelong process of healing and replacing pain with love.

   All this has led me to Micah 6:8 as my life verse.

   "And what does the LORD require of you? To act justly and to love mercy and to walk humbly with your God." (NIV)

   I think this is the Christian agenda we are called to bring to a hurting world. I hope that what I have said has brought glory to God, and has been an encouragement to you. The world needs the love of Jesus. Amen.

You will make known to me the path of life;

In Your presence is fullness of joy;

In Your right hand there are pleasures forever.

Psalm 16:11 (New American Standard Bible)

No king is saved by the size of his army;

　　no warrior escapes by his great strength.

A horse is a vain hope for deliverance;

　　despite all its great strength it cannot save.

But the eyes of the LORD are on those who fear him,

　　on those whose hope is in his unfailing love,

to deliver them from death

　　and keep them alive in famine.

We wait in hope for the LORD;

　　he is our help and our shield.

In him our hearts rejoice,

　　for we trust in his holy name.

Psalm 33:16-21 (New International Version)

Anzar Road

Eleanor Littlestone

This is the story of one small thing that taught me about being God's daughter. There have been many such things, each one precious to me, some of the loveliest treasures I have. They are like jewels, which I can remember during those times when I can't hear God's voice and it looks dark all around, or when I long to remember what it is to be loved intimately by the Lord of all the Universe.

This one happened during spring break of my second year at Cabrillo College. Even by that second year in college, I had not come to terms with having graduated from high school. I suffer from a serious anxiety disorder, and one thing that terrified me to the core was being responsible for figuring out my life, for making momentous and important choices, for going down a good path, for shaping my future. It all felt so dreadfully important, and I felt utterly unqualified for making decisions regarding anything so weighty as my life's course. In any case, that was how it felt to my anxious mind. I yearned for the safety of childhood: the safety of being sheltered under the wings of parents who loved me; most importantly, of having it be their responsibility to figure things out, not mine. The terror was so great, I often felt it would be a relief to be a slave or something similar—to be in some position where I didn't have this dreadful freedom weighing on my shoulders.

I felt shame for not desiring to be independent, for not knowing how to be independent with confidence. After all, our society holds up independence as an ultimate ideal. It tells us we have the grave and exhilarating task of charting our own course, of creating our own identity, of finding our own values, our own niche in the world. And to me, far from being exhilarating, that felt like a burden no human being could possibly bear, a weight beneath which all my bones would be crushed to powder. One tends to internalize the messages of one's society. So I lived those first couple of years out of high school with the feeling— often semi-subliminal—that it was my duty to become happy with being independent. Or if I could not be happy with it, at least to get to the point where I could stand it.

In any case, in this second year of college, I was preparing to go on a six-day retreat over spring break. InterVarsity Christian Fellowship holds spring conferences every year for college students. The spring conference is called "Mark Camp," because it consists of spending seven or eight hours a day studying the Gospel of Mark. The first year, you study the first half of Mark, and the next year, you study the second half. I had gone the previous year and had encountered Jesus powerfully.

But this year, as spring break approached, I was in deep dread of going. I had been warned that the study of the second half of Mark was dark and solemn and intense. Ominous sayings drifted among the InterVarsity students. "Mark Two will wreck you" was one of them. Another was, "In Mark One you watch Jesus kick ass, and in Mark Two Jesus kicks your ass." It was going to be heavy; it was going to involve seeing up close the dark and solemn parts of being a Christian. In the second half of Mark, Jesus said things like, "If anyone wishes to come after Me, he must deny himself, and take up his cross and follow Me. For whoever wishes to save his life will lose it, but whoever loses his life for My sake and the gospel's will save it."[4]

---

4 Mark 8:34b-35 (New American Standard Bible).

I had been afraid, for years, of those sayings of Jesus. And for years I had been hiding from them. It did not help that going on trips always intimidates me. I'm afraid I'll have a panic attack while I'm away, and there will be no one there who understands what's happening to me. I'm afraid of being surrounded by crowds of people I don't know, or don't know very well. To make matters worse, my body has all sorts of quirks, which can make things like six-day conferences kind of an ordeal. For instance, I feel nauseous when I eat salty food, and food at retreat centers has a way of being salty. And when I sit under old tube-style fluorescent lights, I first feel sore in the eyes, then sick in my stomach, then weak in the limbs, and finally I stop being able to carry on a coherent train of thought. (It's a reaction to the fact that they flicker, typically at 120 cycles per second, too fast for the eye to see, but slow enough for the brain to notice.) Furthermore, I get overstimulated ridiculously easily, and when I'm interacting with people all day, the time often comes when I can't process things anymore, and sometimes my eyes even have trouble focusing and I have trouble coming up with words.

I remember lying in bed at night with fears running around in my head, fantasizing about things that would make the trip less intimidating. 'It would really all be okay,' I thought, 'if the room where we were studying was a friendly room, whose architecture felt safe and warm and inviting; and if it didn't have flickery fluorescent lights in the ceiling. It would not be too scary being surrounded by strangers if I were sleeping in a room with friends I trusted, with people I felt safe around. And if the room where we were sleeping felt safe, the kind of place one could nestle down into and rest. It would not be scary if it rained during the retreat. Rain is one of the most comforting things in the world to me: the gentle sound of it falling all around; the clouds covering the big open sky like the shelter of God's wings; the feeling, deep in my bones, that the land is being cared for and nourished and refreshed. And I would not fear the strangers, nor the early mornings, nor the hard sayings of Jesus if, on the trip up there, we went via Anzar Road.'

The thing was, Anzar Road was a lovely treasure of my childhood. When I was growing up, our family vacations often involved traveling from Santa Cruz, across the Central Valley, to the Sierras. And when I was just a baby, my parents found a special and beautiful route for part of the drive. It was a way of avoiding a left turn onto a highway by taking a series of small, quiet roads through the hills around Aromas and into San Juan Bautista. It was a beautiful tradition. Every time we went this way, I would come away remembering that the world is beautiful, life is beautiful, and God is good.

My cousin Laura, who was going to be driving me and a few others to Mark Camp, had proposed we take this route. But some of us needed to get there early (I think for worship band practice), and we thought going along Highway 17 might be faster. But secretly I hoped we could take my beloved childhood route. It would be the richest of treasures to share one of the loveliest things of my childhood with this car full of friends: a jewel lighting up the terrible intimidation of confronting those hard things of Christianity later at camp.

I think I was feeling down about myself for being so terrified of a short little six-day trip away from home, feeling like my fear proved how weak and disabled I was, and how not equipped for adult life. I felt far indeed from achieving that solemn duty of coming to terms with being on my own in the harsh, formidable world.

A couple of days before we were planning to leave, I was praying. Perhaps I was telling God about my fears, about how I loathed myself for being so terrified of this trip and of being an adult in the big harsh world. I don't remember for certain how I prayed, but I do remember that God told me that following Jesus is not about becoming better at doing life alone, but rather about becoming ever more dependent on Him. God spoke to my heart very clearly: "You don't need to strive any longer to be tough enough to go alone in the big harsh world. You will *never* need to do that, because I am your Father."

I had known this intellectually, maybe, but it had not penetrated my heart or gotten past the voices of my own shame for hating independence. But where now was the need for shame, if God didn't even *want* me to like independence, but desired for me to depend on Him fully?

"I want to show you that you are my daughter," God said to me. "I want to teach you to depend on Me. I want to teach you that growing up is not about becoming tough to face things alone. Ask Me for those things which, if they were provided, would make the trip feel safe. Ask Me, and I will provide you with every single one."

It was such a moment of peace. My cold, trembling soul was warmed all over, and I had no doubt that God had spoken to me, that He meant for me to ask for those things, and that He meant to keep His promise. So I asked Him. I did this even though I felt a little trepidation. It seemed odd to ask the King of all the Universe for trifles like going on Anzar Road. I was so used to thinking that I needed to be tough. I was not used to simply putting my hand in Jesus' hand and letting him shelter me in perfect tenderness.

Now on the day we left, I was feeling less certain that God had really had that conversation with me. In any case, I was thinking that soon I would find out if God had made me that promise or not, because in a few hours I would be at Mark Camp. I would know with what roommates I was sleeping, in what room we were studying, and about the other things I had asked for. The lovely thing, though, was that we had already decided to go via Anzar Road. It had turned out that route was just as fast as the alternate one, given how much traffic there was on the alternate route. Laura wrote out the directions, and I promised to help her navigate, since I knew the way by heart and was confident I would recognize every turn we needed to make. So we set out, a happy assemblage of people crowded together in Laura's little red car.

As we drove along, Laura and I were telling the others about the scenic route we were going to take. We told them about the wildflowers blanketing the hills, the goats in the meadows, and the dense, dark eucalyptus grove. I was thinking about how green the hills would be, since it was the height of springtime. On my childhood trips we had always been there in the summer when the hills were dry and brown. Today the grass would be lush and filled with purple filaree flowers and golden swaths of wild mustard blooms.

To get there, we would turn off San Juan Road onto Aromas Road and take various little roads through the tiny town of Aromas to Anzar Road, which went among the hills and finally into San Juan Bautista. But today, as we drove along San Juan Road, we began to realize we had been going for too long.

"Could we have missed the turn?" we asked one another.

"But we couldn't have missed it. We didn't see it yet. I would recognize it. I've been here so many times."

So we went on. There was no Aromas Road in sight, and as the scenery on San Juan Road became less and less familiar, it became clear we had missed our turn. How could we have missed it? We had both been watching for it, and I was sure I would have recognized it.

Laura made some comment about how it was obviously too late to turn around; we were almost at the highway. So all that we had talked about with joy and delight would not be. We would not see the dark eucalyptus grove, nor the goats on the hills. The wild mustard flowers would be there, gold amid the green grass, without us. We would never see whether the marsh was full of water. Silently, in the back seat, I was crying out to God. *'I know I should not feel so sad. It isn't really such a big deal. I always feel so sad about little things. It's only . . . You told me to ask that we would go this way, and you told me that every one of the things I asked for, You would do. You wanted to teach me to depend on You.'* But maybe He hadn't. We could see the turn onto the highway approaching. It was too late. We were careening forward; the drive was continuing; it was just what it was, and I might as well not feel too sad about it. I looked at the billboards along the road, the high concrete retaining walls supporting the road cut. Anzar Road would only have had wildflowers and animals and grass.

Then, somehow, Laura couldn't figure out how to get onto the highway. We could never reconstruct why afterward. On the Google map it looks like the on-ramp was right there. But maybe somehow we had gotten wrongly situated in relation to it, or something. We'll never know. In any case, Laura asked Sam, who was sitting in the front seat, to ask her GPS how to get onto the highway. The GPS, speaking in its animated female voice, instructed Laura to turn onto Cole Road. It was small and bumpy, with aging gray pavement, quietly meandering among meadows and live oaks. I felt my sadness melt. This was not Anzar Road, but it *was* beautiful. Our mistake had not been so bad after all. It had led us to a new thing of beauty, to another scenic route surely as nice as the first one. Maybe this was kind of metaphorical, I found myself thinking. We mess up, and God brings out of our mistake something different that is beautiful. There was one thing that still felt strange, and that was that God had promised we would go on Anzar Road. But I didn't think about it too much and let myself be cheered up, and we drove along talking together about the new scenic route we had found. I did feel that God had saved us, somehow, and in His loving-kindness had not sent us away empty.

Then the GPS spoke again. "Turn right onto Anzar Road."

This was the last thing I had expected to hear.

We came out at almost the beginning of Anzar Road, and there it was, verdant, beautiful, every contour of the hills familiar to my heart. The eucalyptus grove, the mustard, the goats, the marsh . . . they were all there. The GPS had taken us back. It had done what we would not have done ourselves as we plummeted toward the highway, thinking it was too late. If you look at the Google map, you will see that the turnoff onto Cole Road was just moments before the freeway entrance. It was the last road one could have turned onto before reaching the highway.

So I arrived at Mark Camp wrapped in the radiance of God's tenderness and God's sovereignty. As we drove up the winding mountain road to Camp Alta, it was raining. And it was raining while we walked through the dark to the room where my group would be studying. It was the brightest, most cheerful little room imaginable, with wooden walls and a peaked wooden

ceiling and a gas log fireplace in one corner. The lights on the
ceiling were warm in color and not the least flickery. When I
wandered through the room where we would be sleeping, I put
my things down on a random bunk without knowing who would
be anywhere else. And it turned out I was right across from
Amanda and Rachel, two wonderful friends from UC Santa Cruz
InterVarsity.

Later that night, I lay down, the rain all around, the large
room warm and comfortable and kind around me. Under God's
wings I slept, for that moment not afraid to be His child, and
knowing full well I was His child forever.

To tie up the loose ends, I will mention that the Mark
study was wonderful. The journey I took with Jesus about the
sayings of His which had terrified me was luminous and lovely
and changed my walk with God profoundly. And to the delight
of my plant-lover's heart, Camp Alta is in a beautiful place with
a greater diversity of conifers than I had ever seen anywhere. It
often rained while I was there, the rain making sweet sounds on
the roof while we sat inside, safe and warm by the fire, studying
Mark and drinking hot tea. I had no panic attacks, and the people
were wonderful. When we came down the mountain at the end,
in the pouring rain, with majestic clouds crowning the tops of the
mountains, it seemed the whole earth was shouting with glory.
We were radiant, we were triumphant, we were in love with our
God.

Mark Two wrecked me . . . but in the sweetest of ways.

Later I wondered: What if we had found the route by
ourselves? It would have been a lovely drive, but it would not
have been so deeply beautiful. We had failed to find Anzar Road

when we had been sure we could not miss it. But God, in spite of us, was faithful to His promise.

There is a story in *The Giant Golden Book of Elves and Fairies*[5] about a girl named Singeli whose father, out of his great, great love for her, made her a pair of silver slippers. Because of the father's love, the fairies put magic in those slippers that they would guide Singeli "only on bright roads, only on good roads, only on right roads." And a ring of light came out from the slippers, which the wicked trolls did not dare to enter. To me, the magic that guides and protects Singeli is a lot like the Holy Spirit, which God our Father has given us because of His deep and beautiful love. As the story says: "A father's love is like silver slippers, which guide on bright roads, good roads, right roads."

We have a Father who loves us.

Whether you turn to the right or to the left, your ears will hear a voice behind you, saying, "This is the way; walk in it."

Isaiah 30:21 (New International Version)

---

5 "Singeli's Silver Slippers," by Martha Inez Johnson, page 10 in *The Giant Golden Book of Elves and Fairies,* selected by Jane Werner, pictures by Garth Williams © 1951 by Golden Books.

Delight yourself also in the LORD,
And He shall give you the desires of your heart.

Commit your way to the LORD,
Trust also in Him,
And He shall bring it to pass.
He shall bring forth your righteousness
as the light,
And your justice as the noonday.

Rest in the LORD, and wait patiently for Him. . . .
       Psalm 37:4-7 (New King James Version)

There is no fear in love; but perfect love casts out fear, because fear involves torment. . . .

1 John 4:18 (New King James Version)

For God has not given us a spirit of fear, but of power and of love and of a sound mind.

2 Timothy 1:7 (NKJV)

My Walk in Faith

Denby Adamson

My walk in faith really began with my mother, Dorothy Louise Hansen, who was impassioned about God. As a girl, she was involved in her Methodist church helping to run the youth program. But one day she asked her minister, "Do you believe in miracles?" Her minister flatly stated that miracles were for Bible times and not for the present day. My Mom decided that if miracles don't happen then the whole Bible must be a lie, and she became an atheist for a while. But I think in her heart she wrestled with this for a long time and was still ruminating on it when she went to college. She brought up this discussion with her English professor, and she wrote about it and pondered it . . . is prayer real? And miracles too? What is this thing Jesus was talking about? And why are people all into these things if they aren't true? Her English professor suggested that she meet a friend of his, Glenn Clark, who was a creative-writing professor. He had written a best-selling book on prayer. He also ran camps called Camps Farthest Out (CFO),[6] meaning to go farther out with God. So off Mom went to camp to meet Glenn Clark and to search for people of prayer.

At CFO camp, my Mom finally met people who prayed, people of a living faith. Later, back in college in Kentucky, she visited a charismatic church with her roommate and saw people being baptized in the Spirit and everyone shouting "Hallelujah!" She was amazed by what she saw, but she wasn't sure the emotionalism of that church was for her. She did know she

---

6 CFO draws people from around the world and from all branches of Christianity (https://cfonorthamerica.org/). It was founded by Glenn Clark (https://cfointernational.org/sample-page/founder-glenn-clark/).

wanted the experience of the Holy Spirit, a direct connection with God. She told me about her own Holy Spirit experience, which she had on a bus on the way home to New Jersey from Kentucky. She simply said, "Dear God, I would like the Holy Spirit," and in a very quiet, gentle way, while she was looking out over the countryside, she had a sense of God's presence and peace and quiet illumination. She knew that God was real and loved her.

So that was the beginning of her life quest to find people who had a real, active prayer life. People who had gifts of healing, prayer, and prophecy. And people who put their faith into action through service. She looked everywhere.

For a while she became a Quaker, and during World War II she worked alongside other conscientious objectors in mental hospitals. There's a funny story about Mom. She felt she had to do her war duty, and she was put to work in a factory making bombs. But she could not handle the thought of these bombs killing people, so she would pray over them as she was making them. They had to close the factory because the bombs didn't work! So that's why you should not have a conscientious objector working in a bomb factory! Working in the mental hospitals was a much better fit for my Mom, even though it was brutally hard work. She was in charge of 40 patients on her ward. Her tasks included getting them bathed, keeping bedding and clothes clean, overseeing meals, and managing behavior and symptoms.

The Quakers' involvement in mental hospitals during WWII brought about many positive changes in our treatment of the mentally ill. At that time their treatment was little better than something out of a Dickens novel. The patients were mostly people suffering from "shell shock," as they used to call it. But there were also geriatrics and people with depression and schizophrenia, everything mixed in together. Mom was really feisty about the early electric-shock treatments. They used to "really jack 'em up," she said, and Mom just couldn't handle it. The doctor would say, "Hold your patient down!" and she would answer, "*You* hold him down if you think it's so important!" They discovered later that it really *was* too much. The patients would become sort of zombified. Now people are treated more gently.

Later Mom worked with Dorothy Day and the Catholic Workers in the slums of New York. She also worked with Frank Laubach and his organization for world literacy, and many other famous people. When I was a child she would invite them to our house and to our community—visitors like Brother Mandus from England, who had a gift of healing, and Buckminster Fuller, an inventor and visionary. There were also the quirky people— artists and writers and free thinkers.

Anyway, that's Mom. She wasn't afraid to stand up to people of power and to stand up for what she believed. She was tenacious and single-focused about God. That's all she talked about night and day. But she was not a conventional Christian. I would say she was a missionary to the bohemians. She hitchhiked to the West Coast in the 40s, along the way attending a seminar with Albert Schweitzer in Colorado. Eventually she made it to California. She checked out a compassionately run farm for the mentally ill in Los Gatos and worked there for a while as a cook (Mom hated to cook). Then she ended up in Big Sur and stayed for about seven years. She arrived at Deetjen's Big Sur Inn bare-foot and with her hair down. They said, "You belong!" and they gave her a job. That is how she came to California.

Mom believed in hitchhiking, and wherever we went we picked up hitchhikers. She was never afraid; she was always excited about people. For her, finding the jewel of hope, the bit of faith, the wonderful kernel of truth in each person was a treasure hunt for the presence of God. She felt it was her duty to nourish that seed of faith by encouraging and affirming that person. She brought the subject with everyone around to God somehow. She did have a few negative experiences as a young woman hitchhiking alone, but she would talk about God and the men would give up. In one instance, when she was at gunpoint, Mom looked at the man and said, "What would your mother think if she saw you now?" And he put the gun away and let her out of the truck.

Mom brought many people to Christ, not by quick conversions, but by being with them, quietly loving them every day, helping them with their trials, and being an example of strength and faith. Wherever we went, my Mom would find people in need or someone "interesting," and then she would say, "I met the most amazing person!" It happened so often that sometimes I'd just roll my eyes and say to myself, "Oh, no, who is she on to now!"

My childhood was full of saints, lots of people who had demonstrable gifts of prayer. I always knew that our lives were different from other people's. For one thing, I always seemed to be hanging out with adults. I am basically an only child as my oldest half brother, Richard, is almost 18 years older than me. We did not do mainstream cultural things like watch football games or barbecue, and my parents never drank. Still, it was odd to me that other people did not seem to know about or experience God the way we did.

My birth father died when I was eight months old; he drowned at Jade Cove in Big Sur. As a single mother, my Mom dragged me along with her everywhere, to prayer groups, seminars, college, and church. My earliest spiritual memory is of being in a Quaker church when I was about two—tiptoeing through the church in this amazing nourishing silence. I remember that it blessed me so much—the presence of God in that quiet and peace. Quakers feel that you meet God within yourself, so the whole service is about being quiet, meeting God, and listening to what He tells you. Occasionally someone will stand up and say something inspirational.

We were living in Monterey at the time. One prayer group leader, named Bessie, was a constant in our lives. Whenever there was a big decision, Mom would pray with Bessie. My memory of Bessie is of a tiny lady with enormous glasses. When just chatting she would complain about this and that. I sometimes used to think, "Hurry up, Bessie—start praying!" because when she was praying she was a totally different person. You felt the peace and presence of Jesus. She would start prophesying and it was amazing. It was almost as if by starting with complaining she wanted to reassure you that she was human.

When I was three years old, my Mom remarried and we moved to Marin. We tried to continue with the Quaker meetings, but the only meeting house was in San Francisco. My Dad commuted there every day and didn't want to do it on weekends, so we stayed in Marin. We found a family church, a house church right near our home. I loved it. It was a delightful Spanish-style house, where the minister was a lady named Paula who spent her time in prayer. In fact her whole life was prayer. She never went far from the phone, so she could be available to pray with people in need. (This was before cell phones.) It was such a loving, blessed little community, with a Sunday school. We acted out Bible stories and played in the beautiful garden. But best of all, we had my Mom as a teacher and Paula, who was always talking to God, always telling us to turn our eyes away from our problems and put them back on God. She would say, "I was praying this morning, and God told me such and such. . . ." After experiencing this kind of church, it was hard to go to a conventional church, where God seemed so distant and people did not really seem to believe. I ended up developing a prejudice against regular churches because my house church was so sweet.

My Mom believed that God talks to us in dreams. She always encouraged me to remember my dreams. In the mornings over breakfast, we often shared our dreams and talked about what they might mean. When I was around nine, I started dreaming about churches. In my dream, I would walk up to a church, and it would be like crackers, and I would eat them. There were all these churches, and I would eat the churches! I wasn't sure what this meant. I had other dreams in which Jesus was somewhere in the dream, always my friend. He was always protecting me from something bad in the dream, which I now believe was fear. Sometimes He was a little boy who played with me, and sometimes He was just somewhere in the house. I had many dreams about Jesus being my friend protecting me. When I was ten, I had a series of dreams about a broken-down mansion that was covered with moss. In the last one, I was walking across some rubble and there was a driveway. I saw Jesus in His adult form in white robes, a traditional image of Jesus. He was by a white pickup truck—I don't know what the white pickup truck means! He said to me, "In three years you shall have a baby." I was 10! I was confused by that! A short time later, my Mom took me to a conference where they had a children's workshop on dreams. I went to the workshop, and two of us shared our dreams. The workshop leader told me that babies in dreams are a gift from God. She told me I should pray about what gift to ask from God. She also told me that eating churches meant that I should, or would, partake of churches. This was a kind of prophecy, as at the time I did not feel comfortable in mainstream churches.

About this time I often heard my Mom talking on the phone, either counseling people or just talking about spiritual things. One day they were talking about the Holy Spirit and the experience of speaking in tongues. Some people didn't think it was true. Mom defended it as biblical, and the conversation went back and forth. I heard about the Holy Spirit experience, and I thought, "That's what I want!" I waited three years to have this experience.

Every summer we went to CFO (Camps Farthest Out), and there I had contact with people of all different faiths and perspectives. When we came to camp that year, I knew that I was going to ask for the gift of the Holy Spirit. I was 13. I was in a group of six boys and six girls, and we decided to ask together. This was without parental supervision. We thought our parents were not with it. 'They're not trusting,' we thought. 'They don't know. We're just going to go out there and ask for the Holy Spirit and see what happens.' So we did! And within a few minutes we were filled with the Spirit. One adult somehow snuck in, I'm not sure how, but she seemed to have the gift of knowledge, and she said, "Jesus is telling me that your sins are forgiven." My rational mind was thinking, 'You know, I'm 13 and I don't really have that many sins. What can I have done?' But it just broke me open, and I felt the presence of God. I was filled with His presence, and I was singing and praising God for the whole night—in fact into the week. That kept me going for quite a while.

But it was like an addiction; it was almost like a drug because the next year I wanted the same experience. Then I realized that after you have these mountain-top experiences, you have to put into practice what you learned, so I joined my parents' prayer group. I felt a bit embarrassed to join my parents' prayer group, but I did, and I started praying and meditating for 15 minutes every morning and evening. I continued listening to my dreams, and I started using spiritual affirmations during the day, so I could keep focused on what God would have me do.

It was very healing because I was a spacey child. I was delicate in some ways. My Mom's great gift was listening to me. I would come home sometimes and say, "Oh there are so many problems at school. I just can't deal with it." Sometimes I got sick when I felt overwhelmed. My Mom occasionally let me stay home from school, and I would go walking in the woods. I would bring a book, something inspirational like Corrie ten Boom or *God's Smuggler* or one of Glenn Clark's books—something that was easy to read and would take my mind off my problems. Then I would just sit there, watching the sun go across the sky and looking at the tapestry of trees. I would let the stillness slowly seep in and feel the presence of God. I found life at school challenging, but this constant meditation really helped. It healed me. It helped me be able to focus on school work. It helped me not to be so drained or affected by people and my surroundings. It enabled me to bring the presence of God with me wherever I was during the day.

So back to my prejudice against churches. I had some negative experiences when I encountered people from a more traditional Christian background. They often seemed to distrust things like getting quiet, listening to God, and hearing His answers. They would say, "You have to be so careful, the devil this, and the devil that. . . ." They would challenge me by asking suspiciously, "Are you saved?" I always felt their fear—a legalistic fear of what would happen if you didn't follow the right rules. They made me feel like I didn't fit in and I wasn't good enough. They wanted me to say that I had "accepted Jesus as my Savior," but Jesus had *always* been my friend and confidant. It felt so trite the way they used some formula to reach Him.

For some Christians going to church was merely a moral or social tradition. These people did not seem to really believe in God or have a personal relationship with Him. And some Christians used the Bible as a weapon to prove that whatever *you* said was wrong and *they* were right. I never felt comfortable in any church other than my own home church. I often felt closer to God in the woods. But God had other plans. . . .

In high school I did not have a community of youth to fellowship with, but I did go to CFO summer camps and retreat weekends. Sometimes I went to six camps a year. I also began to pray for the right husband. I wanted to find someone who was as devoted to God as I was, someone who made me feel safe. I became very interested in healing, prayer, and alternative medicine. I went to an alternative high school, and in my sophomore year, I got credit for a four-month trip through Mexico and Guatemala with my parents and a friend. We would stop our VW camper and have prayer and meditation wherever we were. On that trip I discovered a Seventh-day Adventist naturopathic school that seemed very cool, and I decided to go there after I finished high school. It seemed like a safe environment. No dating was allowed, and it was Christian.

I got a massage certificate after I graduated from high school and then went to the naturopathic school in Guatemala. In the Seventh-day Adventist world all my uncomfortable church feelings were taken up a notch. The Seventh-day Adventists were sincere but suspicious of me and my relationship to God. Most of the Bible studies were basic evangelical doctrine, but there was all this Ellen White[7] stuff—some of it good and some I could not agree with. All this was coupled with being far away from home and in a different culture, eating vegetarian, having to wear dresses everyday, having arms and knees covered, speaking a different language, and keeping a strict Sabbath from Friday night to Saturday night.

Then a major disaster intensified the whole experience. Three days after I arrived, a 7.9-magnitude earthquake hit Guatemala, and 28,000 people died. It was like being on the wrong side of the TV screen. Being surrounded by Seventh-day Adventist doctrine, doing Bible studies night and day while aftershocks continued, seemed to intensify my companions' fear. They thought the Lord was coming and nobody felt ready. The Bible studies became more intense. They culminated in a paganism study, which left me feeling like the rug had been pulled out from under me—basically birthdays, wedding rings, Christmas and Easter celebrations were all considered pagan. With all this intensity morning and night, I just wanted to be in the woods by myself on the Sabbath. But after a few weeks I felt God telling me to go to church. So I went back into the church, which made everyone else feel more calm about me, less suspicious of me—this Quaker person who talked to God.

I did become a Seventh-day Adventist for a while, but I think it was through coercion. It was just such an intense

7 An early leader of the Seventh-day Adventist Church, and a leading figure in American vegetarian history.

experience. When the middle of the year came along, I wanted to go to the first international CFO conference in England. I had decided to go there long before I went to Guatemala, but the Seventh-day Adventists were not interested in letting me go. Their agenda was to turn me into a medical missionary, and I almost went that route. But somehow they let me go. They loaded me down with Seventh-day Adventist literature, which I carried in a huge back pack with all my stuff.

Being a Seventh-day Adventist actually saved me on that trip. I was getting harassed on the border by the bus drivers and by a gang of guys that wanted to take me to the beach for the night. I was 19 at the time—a woman alone. While I was talking to an older gentleman about Seventh-day Adventist doctrine, a missionary heard me. He took me under his wing and to the one place in Mexico City where I could stay for a dollar—the Seventh-day Adventist mission house. He rescued me from all this pestering abuse, which had already caused me to miss my plane.

So I got to England. My Mom met me there, and we went to the CFO conference. She started talking, and she found an amazing person. (She usually does!) This amazing person told her, "Oh, you know, my boyfriend is playing in a band and you really should meet him. He is a wonderful Christian guy." I wasn't paying much attention. I was just listening with half an ear while listening to speakers at the camp. I was also busy trying to get rid of another guy, a relief worker who had been in Guatemala and was also at the conference. I was trying to tell him that, "No, there really isn't going to be anything happening between us." So I was kind of distracted. Meanwhile, the wonderful Christian guy's girlfriend picked him up from his rock concert. Unbeknownst to me, she told him that he was going to fall in love with me. Then she brought him to the CFO conference.

His name was Ian. When I met him, he looked me in the eye. He took off his glasses and looked me in the eye. And I thought, 'How can I arrange another meeting with this guy?' I suggested that we go to the Mary Light prayer group. (Mary Light[8] was an old-time CFO speaker from Canada who had a gift for prayer.) He said, "Okay," so we met at the Mary Light prayer group and the electricity started flying. I was sitting next to him, and it was like "zzzzzzzzzz," a tangible electricity. Soon he told his girlfriend that he *had* fallen in love with me, then immediately came and asked me to marry him. That was about three days after I had first met him. He wanted to go off to get a ring, and I was saying, "No no, Seventh-day Adventists don't believe in rings." Anyway, I put my plane ticket away and stayed a little longer. We didn't have much time to talk. He was working at a Christian home for the mentally ill, which had clients with a very broad range of problems. There was a man who had killed someone in a bar fight, someone who was a biker type, all kinds of characters. I slept in the women's dorm with someone who seemed to be developmentally disabled and wet her bed.

One day I was alone with Ian, floating along some country road, talking about all the things we believed and the music we liked. I said, "We don't believe the same things." He was a Baptist and I, a free-thinking experiential Californian Christian. He said, "You know, we may not agree on everything. But look at people's fruits. Watch a person's fruits and you will know if Christ is within them. Look at someone's fruits and you will know who they are." I instantly felt safe. He was a Christian

---

8 https://www.cfoclassicslibrary.org/library?speaker_id=17

without fear. I was impressed. I felt secure knowing that Ian loved me for who I was, and not for something I said or was doing.

I returned to Guatemala to finish my term and then went back to America. I tried to go to Sonoma State University to pursue a degree in creative arts therapy, but I had hepatitis from being in Guatemala and was not able to complete the program. I then went to live at a retreat center owned by a friend of my Mom's. It was on Alba Road in the Santa Cruz Mountains. After nine months of separation, Ian followed me there. About eight women eventually joined me for an intensive training program using movement, music, and creative expression for healing, as well as meditation and journaling. We each had our own rooms in the beautiful center in the redwoods. I was still recovering from the hepatitis, so this was a perfect time for healing and reflection. But I was also the youngest trainee, and Ian the only man, so this made for some interesting times. Ian spent a lot of time working in the woods, not being able to handle all the sharing that went on between the women!

About four years later, Ian and I were married. After our marriage, Ian said, "We need to go to church." But I was thinking, 'No! I feel more comfortable in the woods.' Then one day God spoke to me, clear as a bell.

He said, "Well, Denby, where do people look for Me?"

"They look in the yellow pages," I answered.

"And what is in the yellow pages?"

"Churches!" I said, "Okay God, I will go to church."

We went to a Methodist church in Boulder Creek. We finally found a church that we could handle together. We began helping with singing and worship. One Sunday I gave my testimony, and one of the church members that I had found intimidating came up to me and said, "You sure are religious!" I was totally gobsmacked. I had been intimidated by them and now they were telling me that I was religious—it was so funny. God has mysterious ways of getting us to do His will, and we just have to trust Him.

Eventually that church had problems with their pastor, and Ian began looking for another church. He wanted a peaceful, safe place for the kids. I was busy teaching Sunday school and helping out with our old church and the community there. For several Sundays, Ian visited the Bonny Doon Church. At that time the congregation was tiny, but he felt that this was the place for us. He kept telling me that he felt drawn to Bonny Doon. It was hard for me to leave, but eventually it became obvious that the problems in our old church were not going to disappear, so we left and started coming to Bonny Doon on Sunday. About the same time, John Burke became the new pastor and many more families joined the church, including families with kids.

There have been so many answers to prayer and so many miracles in our lives. For example, we didn't have enough money to buy a bed, and a bed came down our driveway. In the beginning Ian didn't have any work and we just prayed for everything. Everything was supplied to us, even a place to live.

We had always been attracted to a house on Alba Road. It was the one place on the road where we noticed the sun shining. We used to look at the house, and we would say to ourselves, "Some day. . . ." When we were talking about marriage, we said, "Let's go check it out," but we never did. After we were married, we were living in my Mom's basement with two dogs. The puppies were pulling all the plants out of Mom's pots and creating mayhem and destruction. Ian was going door to door selling art and looking for work. We started praying for a house.

We wanted a place that was beautiful, that had space around it. We wanted a place that was affordable, and a place where we could raise a family. One day my Mom's friend Kay, from the retreat center, called and said, "Come on down. There is this care-taking job on Alba Road." So we went, and we saw that it was the same house we had always been attracted to. We went down the driveway and the woman said, "Well, we can't pay you very much. We can only pay you $150 dollars a month." We kept saying, "Well, we could pay you rent," and she kept saying, "We can't pay you very much." By the third time she said, "We can't pay you very much," we said, "Fine, we'll take it!" It was perfect because Ian was unemployed at the time, just doing odd jobs, as he was finding it difficult to find work as a non-citizen.

That house supported Ian's beginning work at Mateo Lodge,[9] where he started at $500 a month as a part-time coordinator. It enabled him to build the organization into what it is today. That house supported me being able to homeschool my kids, and it supported me being able to take care of my mother. We lived in that house for 35 years. A long time ago God promised me that the house would eventually be ours, and just this last year (2019) our son, Danny, was able to buy it.

So God is good. Delight yourself in the Lord, and He will give you the desires of your heart. Trust the Lord and be not afraid, no matter what happens.

On the following page is one of Denby Adamson's favorite songs. It is #34 in CFO Sings, copyright 1982 by the Association of Camps Farthest Out, and is reprinted here with permission.

---

9 https://www.smc-connect.org/locations/mateo-lodge-inc

In The Secret of His Presence

Sung to the tune "Annie Laurie"
by Alicia A. Spottiswoode

In the secret of His Presence,
My soul has found repose;
And a voice within the silence
Transmutes to joy my woes.
Here I lay my burdens down,
And deny the power of sin,
And I'm conscious of the Presence
Of the Christ who dwells within.

Be still, my soul, and hearken,
Let all the earth be still,
While the Master whispering softly
Reveals to me His will.
And the still small voice I hear,
When freed from mortal din,
For I'm conscious of the Presence
Of the Christ who dwells within.

Eye hath not seen such beauty,
Ear hath not heard such tone.
Heart ne'er conceived such splendor
As Christ to me makes known.
Oh, would that all mankind,
This priceless gem might win,
To be conscious of the Presence
Of the Christ who dwells within.

The Boy with the Hole
In His Heart

Ian Adamson

I was born three years after the end of the Second World War, in a London still recovering from the ravages of conflict. I can remember as a child taking ration coupons to buy a stick of butter or some other luxury; however, I never had a sense that our family lacked anything—such was the unconditional love that my sister Wendy (two years my senior) and I grew up in.

My father was an orphan born in 1916. His father had been killed in the First World War. When he was in his 70's, my father found out that his mother's name was Edith Rogers and his given name was Leslie Brandon Rogers, so in fact I came close to being a Mr. Rogers.

Dad and Mum met each other in London and worked in service at the Houses of Parliament. They actually lived in the servants' quarters in Big Ben. When I was born I had heart trouble, but I was never concerned about that growing up. My parents never sheltered me, so I grew up doing everything, including lots of sports. At the age of 11, I had major heart surgery, which was successful.

My upbringing, as I remember it, was very happy. I grew up on a large housing estate called Harold Hill (named for King Harold) with many friends. We loved fishing and playing soccer. One day, one of my friends told me about a youth center run by a local church. It sounded fun, so I went along. This youth activity included church attendance. It was the first time in my life that I was exposed to anything religious, although both my Mum and Dad were deeply spiritual, and my father often sang hymns.

I can remember thinking when I heard Christians talk about their faith that it was something outside my experience. I felt they had a different relationship with God, and it intrigued me. I was a very innocent, open, and honest 11-year-old, and I remember being impressed with the love those simple Christians showed to me and others. I was a young man in a hurry, always turning up just as the service was about to begin. I would leave my bike outside the church, and every time, one of the elders would carry it into the church, so it would not get stolen. Our little church had no paid minister; in fact, everyone did things just for the love of it.

It was the second time I heard the gospel message that I responded. I simply asked Jesus to enter into my life. That changed everything in profound, quiet ways. First, I felt the presence of God enter my being. It was all love, of an eternal quality. I was filled with love for all creation. Several other things happened. The scriptures talk about living water that satisfies us. I felt I had found the meaning of life: to love. It gave me great joy and peace. I was also given a great love of the Bible. I insisted that my mother read a chapter to me every night, and she was happy to do it.

So my life was changed, and I was full of love for all creation. When you are in this blissful state, you feel compelled to share because you want others to be as happy. This was the beginning of my Christian experience. I am very grateful for the reality of it. Therefore I was never threatened by people who held different beliefs. I never felt I had to convert them, just to love them.

As I approach the later years of my life, I look back on my decision to do my best to follow Christ as the greatest decision of my life. It has led me to the fulfillment of what the scriptures call "the desires of my heart." I feel so blessed to have been born into love and to experience Divine Love. I have felt God's presence in all the important decisions of my life and have experienced His faithfulness. I look forward to the next chapter of my human adventure knowing that God is Love and that He walks with me.

Ian Adamson and Aaron Mohamed lead us in worship with their guitars, starting with a special time of singing for the children. We are including here two of our children's favorite songs, "Bee Bop" and "The Fruit of the Spirit." It is not uncommon for the children to request, and for us to sing with all the actions, these same two songs every Sunday for weeks on end.

Bee Bop (action song)[10]

I've got love in my heart, wait and see
>   (Make a heart shape with your hands, over your heart.)

bop bop bop bop bop bop bop bop Bee Bop
>   (Stoop with hands on knees for all the bops. Jump in the
>   air with your hands raised and shout when you get to the
>   Bee Bop.)

I'm so happy, I could fly, and I know the reason why;
>   (Spread both arms out for wings and pretend to fly.)

I've got Jesus in my heart, wait and see
>   (Put both arms above you with first fingers
>   outstretched when you say, "Jesus," then make a heart
>   shape over your heart when you get to the word "heart.")

bop bop bop bop bop bop bop bop Bee Bop
>   (Same as the first time.)

Sing the second verse, "I've got joy . . ." very loudly.
Start the third verse, "I've got peace. . ." very quietly, but when
you get to the Bee Bop, jump and shout loudly, as in the first two
verses.

---

10 As far as we can tell this song is in the public domain. The composer is
unknown.

Bee Bop

The Fruit of the Spirit[11]

Instructions: Have the children choose a fruit and invent an action for it. For example, if they pick a lemon, they might decide to make a round shape with their hands to represent it. Sing, "The fruit of the Spirit is not a lemon," then make the hand signal and shout, "Lemon!" where the x's appear in the music. Continue with the rest of the song.

Pick another fruit and start over. It is perfectly okay for the fruit of the Spirit not to be a pizza, or a train car, or anything else the children come up with. Have fun!
Ian plays this in the key of C.

```
     C                            G
The fruit of the Spirit's not a _____,
     C                            D
The fruit of the Spirit's not a _____,
G     C                      F
If you want to be a _____, you might as well hear it,
     C      G      C           D
You can't be a fruit of the Spirit. 'Cuz the fruits are
F             D                          C
love, joy, peace, patience, kindness, goodness, faithfulness,
G             C      G           C  G  C
gentleness, and self control,  (repeat) . . . self control.
```

11 This song is by Uncle Charlie and is reproduced here with permission. See www.unclecharlie.com. This and many similar songs are available for free on Uncle Charlie's VBG kids app. See .www.ValuedByGod.com

The Fruit of the Spirit

Uncle Charlie

Thy word is a lamp unto my feet, and a
light unto my path.

Psalm 119:105 (King James Version)

The Story of My Faith

Frauke Zajac

The gift of faith was given to me through my father, Clemens Ruether. Father grew up on a farm in a small village in Germany. He was the youngest of seven boys and watched all of his brothers being ordered to go off to war. One of them did not return; the others came back severely wounded physically and emotionally. My father spent most of his days accompanying my grandfather to work, since his mother suffered from a broken heart after seeing her children's lives destroyed by war.

When my father was 14 years old, my grandparents were no longer able to care for him. They sent him off to another town where he apprenticed with a carpenter. Learning a trade as an apprentice was a common practice in Germany. He worked for room and board without much other means of support. However, he discovered a Catholic organization for young craftsmen, called Kolpingswerk after its founder, Adolf Kolping. This organization provided spiritual and practical support for the young tradesmen.

My father joined Kolpingswerk and enjoyed a place that offered spiritual nourishment, social engagement (such as theater groups), business and educational classes, and hot meals and fellowship at the end of a workday. Here he learned about ways to further his education. He moved up in the trades, became a master carpenter, and took night classes to learn about business. Through a colleague he met my Mom, who with her bright spirit brought new joy to his life. With much hard work and support from my mother and her close-knit family, my father eventually became president of a large furniture company. My parents were able to move to a beautiful place, my hometown, and build a lovely home for their family.

My father was not a person to preach much about faith, but his way of living was a testament to his Christian values and beliefs. I have never heard my Dad raise his voice; he is always respectful and kind to all people and especially supportive of the weak members of his community. He was a tough but fair boss. When one of his workers came to work drunk, he laid him off but assured him he could resume his employment once he got help. One of the first things he did after taking over the furniture company was to raise the wages of women so they were equal to those of the men.

Whenever there was a dispute amongst family or friends, he would advise but not condemn anyone, since we all have our own flaws. I realized that a lot of his values are biblical principles. For example, honesty was very important to him, as well as contentment and appreciation for what you have. He was a model of working with discipline and then enjoying and sharing the fruit of your labor with your family and others. He always looked for opportunities to give a helping hand to weaker people around him. He enjoyed the blessings in his life, but did not like to see greed in society. His overall attitude and one of his favorite sayings was, "Make the best of any situation and circumstance you find yourself in."

During some very difficult times in my life, my father called me every day, calmly listened to the situation, took every aspect into account, and suggested the best way forward for every person involved. The last sentence in our conversation was always, "Let's make the best of it."

My father truly has the fruits of the spirit: love, joy, peace, patience, kindness, goodness, faithfulness, gentleness, and self control.[12]

When I was a young child, our family would go to church together on Sundays, followed by a nice meal at a restaurant. That way my Mom did not have to cook one day a week, and the family could enjoy time together.

I loved to stand next to my father in church and hear him sing the hymns, which he knew by heart. When I go back home to Germany, it is still special for me to stand next to him in our church and hear him sing those familiar hymns.

When I went to high school, we had a wonderful religion teacher who helped me explore my faith in more depth. Religion was one of my favorite school subjects. I also sang in a choir and played the flute in church with friends who played the piano and the cello. Music was always a special gift to me.

During college I moved away from my faith. I did not return to it for many years, until I had a young son. I thought he needed to learn that there is more to this life than the material side. Little did I know, I was really the one who needed to get back to my faith. One of my friends in Bonny Doon suggested that I accompany her to Bonny Doon Church, and she mentioned that there was a nice choir I could join. I had turned very far away from my faith at this point, but I wanted my son to be exposed to the church, so we attended a few services and felt very welcomed by the Bonny Doon congregation. The choir was a joyful group, and there I met a special friend, Marion, a fellow German. Soon I found in this little church a family away from home, much like the family my father had found in the Kolpingswerk group when he was an apprentice.

---

12 See Galatians 5:22-23 (New American Standard Bible)

My father now wishes he had a small loving church and tells me that Bonny Doon Church is worth more than gold or silver. I feel like a circle is closing. My father was given support and faith by a small Christian group, which he passed on to me, and now I get to carry my experience from a small loving Christian community back to him for his support in old age.

God had the perfect plan. He placed two German people in Bonny Doon to bring me back to my faith. One friend, who happened to be from a small town near my hometown, brought me to church, and the other, my good friend Marion, became my "German sister in Christ" in a country far away from home. "God is good!"—as Marion would say!

I live far from my family in Germany, but perhaps I needed to travel this far in order to find my faith again through this loving community of Christians. Joining Bonny Doon Church has blessed my family here and my family in Germany. It is sometimes a challenge to be far from my home country, but taking my father's advice, I will make the best of it—with God and my church family by my side. And as to my son, he has become a loving young man working in the medical field, whose desire to serve people was awakened by the love of God and this little church.

Prodigal

Tom Ray

Hi, my name is Tom, and I am a grateful believer in Jesus Christ who struggles with alcohol, drugs, codependency, and emotional issues related to childhood dysfunction.

Growing up in the Campbell and Los Gatos area during the 60's was quite an experience. As a young boy I was full of energy and very active, so naturally I loved sports.

Attending a strict Catholic school, I soon learned what corporal punishment meant. The nuns would apply the board of education to the seat of correction frequently.

My home life was very volatile. My parents fought a lot, and at night I would wake up to the sounds of them yelling and screaming at each other. My mother divorced my Dad when I was in the second grade. I have two older brothers and one younger sister, so my mother had her work cut out for her.

While she worked, our home was a war zone. I was always fighting with my older brother Chris. One day after school I came home to find my electric guitar in pieces. Chris was jealous that I was learning the guitar in school and tried to keep me from practicing. Many other painful things took place, and by the time I was in the sixth grade, I made a decision never to forgive my brother for all the harm he had done to me.

When I got into junior high, I was in the party crowd—alcohol, marijuana, and rock & roll were the way I dealt with the pain of my dysfunctional family life. Getting high became my number one priority in life. By the time I got into high school, I was too much trouble for my mother, so I moved in with my Dad. This was not a good experience. He partied every night and lived a life of excess.

My view of God was shaped by my Catholic school experience. I was afraid of God and thought He was ready to pound me if I did anything wrong, just like the nuns.

During my senior year in high school, I moved back home with my mother and sister in Campbell. Their lives had changed drastically. They were attending the Calvary Chapel in San Jose, and both experienced the wonderful love of Jesus. Soon after moving back in with them, I began to notice gospel tracts placed around the house in strategic places. The tracts had sports themes on the outside covers, so they got my attention. As I read them, I learned for the first time that I was a sinner. The scriptures in the tracts convicted me big time. I became aware of the emptiness in my heart, and how I was trying to fill the gigantic void in my life with alcohol, drugs, and promiscuity. I soon began to hate those gospel tracts! I came to realize that I was indeed separated from God, and with my own eyes I saw the transformation of life in my mother and sister.

After graduating from high school, I began to work at a local grocery store. One of my party friends from high school, Mark, got involved with a group of guys that were really into LSD and the whole Jim Morrison genre. They were experimenting with the psychedelic drug and taking many doses. One day I stopped by Mark's apartment and saw a note from the Santa Clara County coroner's office pinned to his front door. It was addressed to his parents. It read: You need to come to the coroner's office to identify the body of your son.

Mark had died from circumstances related to the heavy use of LSD. It was like a ton of bricks fell on me! I was completely in shock. I had never known a person who had died. All of a sudden the realness of my own mortality was weighing heavily on me. Numerous thoughts plagued my mind, like, "I am going to die one day, and I am definitely not ready!"

Desperately trying to make sense of it all, my thoughts went to my old Catholic church, my only point of reference to God. So I immediately drove over and went inside. I knelt at the front and began to mourn over the death of Mark. I cried out to God, and to my utter amazement He heard me!

Soon after this, God began to work in many unmistakable ways in my life. A few of my co-workers began inviting me to church. I attended a Sunday school class for the college age. As soon as I walked into the meeting and heard the songs of praise and the Bible being taught, I knew I had found what I was searching for: the Lord Jesus Christ, the King of kings and Lord of lords.

So on March 6, 1983, during the evening service at Crossroads Bible Church, I went forward during the altar call and prayed to receive Jesus Christ to be the Lord of my life. I was 20 years old.

As a new believer I was encouraged to read the Bible daily. Reading through the book of Genesis for the first time as a Christian, I was tremendously moved by the story of Joseph and his brothers. When Joseph was a youth, his brothers mistreated him badly, even selling him into slavery. The Lord began to minister to my heart when I read this, and as the story unfolded, I felt a deep inner pain related to my family turmoil. When I got to the part where Joseph, as the ruler in Egypt, reveals himself to his brothers and speaks the words "You meant evil against me; but God meant it for good."[13] my heart was pierced; this verse was an astounding revelation to me. The years I had suffered at

---

13 Genesis 50:20 (New King James Version).

the hands of my brother were for a reason. They were extremely crucial in bringing me to salvation.

A few years passed and my family moved up north to Eugene, Oregon. I followed shortly thereafter in 1985. I lived there for about 10 years and endured some disasters that were related to a dysfunctional church I attended. At that church I met a Christian woman, and we were engaged a year later. The church revealed how controlling and dysfunctional it was as the wedding day approached. This created a wedge between my fiancée and me, and our relationship dissolved.

I did not deal well with these adversities and fell away from the Lord. I blamed God for the many things that had taken place and fell back into alcohol to numb my inner turmoil. I was completely miserable.

During phone calls, my sister prayed for me and tried to encourage me in the Lord. I hit rock bottom when I lost a great job that had opportunities for advancement. Life was completely out of control and unmanageable. All my pursuits met with disaster.

Every hope I had for my future was shattered, and I could see nothing good ahead. I moved back to the Bay Area and lived a life of sin, my heart a million miles away from God. Then the Lord brought Al and Vivian Mendoza into my life. Al and Vivian are small-group leaders with Celebrate Recovery in a church in San Jose. I lived across the street from them.

One hot summer night there was a really loud party at a neighbor's house. Broken beer bottles, shouting, loud music, and ruckus filled the night air. I observed Al walking over to the area and talking with the neighbors. The next thing I knew, I heard yelling and screaming as a group of intoxicated thugs jumped Al, beat him to the ground, and kicked him while he was on the asphalt. Immediately a large group of people ran over to rescue him, and soon the ambulance and police arrived.

After awhile I went over to Al's and spoke with him. His face was badly beaten; he had lacerations on his forehead, eyebrows, and nose. There was severe swelling over most of his face. His nose was swollen, and he had injuries to his elbows, arm, and leg. He was in a lot of pain, but conducted himself with a depth of character I had never witnessed. No anger. No revenge. No hostility. He was a tremendous example of God's grace at work in a person's life.

A few days later I stopped by Al and Vivian's. They invited me into their home and began to minister the love of the Lord to me. Al reassured me of God's unconditional love for me. He told me that no matter what I had done, God still loved me and was willing to forgive me for the many years I had fallen away. His heartfelt prayers and preaching began to impact my life. I had been running away from God for years. God was reaching out to me through Al and Vivian.

At night the memories of Al's beating would come to mind. I felt like the Lord was saying to me, "Tom, do you see the scars and wounds my son Jesus suffered as a substitute for you? Jesus bore the beating and punishment, and was wounded for you!"

My sins were paid for by His pain and torture. Within the depths of my heart I was touched and sensed a healing taking place. I was broken before the Lord, lamenting over the bad decision I had made to return to a life of sin. The Lord was reaching out to me in my backslidden state.

In the days that followed, Al and Vivian were instrumental in my returning to the Lord. In Galatians 6:1 (New King James Version) it says, "If a man is overtaken in any trespass, you who are spiritual restore such a one in a spirit of gentleness, considering yourself lest you also be tempted." This is exactly what happened. God worked through Al Mendoza to restore my life to Him.

In the months that followed, Al and Vivian invited me to Celebrate Recovery. At first I thought I had too many problems and was very ashamed. They explained to me that at Celebrate Recovery each person has areas they are working on, and each person is a work in progress. After many months of making lame excuses I finally went! On January 1, 2010, there was a New Year's Day meeting at Family Community Church in San Jose.

I began to attend Celebrate Recovery at Family Community Church and participated in the small groups. This is where I met Ron. He is a small-group leader. When I heard Ron and the others share about their struggles, I felt more at ease. I was reassured that all that was shared in the small group would remain strictly confidential. This provided an atmosphere where men could open up and share exactly what was in their hearts. The small group was a tremendous blessing. A step study group was scheduled to begin soon. I was encouraged to sign up for it. I did, and Ron agreed to be my sponsor.

As I worked through the steps, God brought up the family issues that took place while I was growing up, and the resentments I held against my brother Chris. The Lord was working in my heart and helping me to understand that He wanted to heal the many wounds that still festered below the surface.

I have heard some people in step study group[14] say that they have two or three things they are going to take with them to the grave

---

14 A group of co-dependents working through the 12 steps (www.celebraterecovery.com/resources/cr-tools/12steps).

concerning their 4th[15] step inventory. But my sponsor said that I would get out of the step study exactly as much as I was willing to put in. So I resolved in my heart not to exclude anything from my past as I worked through the steps. I am so glad I did! There is nothing more freeing than being healed from your past. The step study group has made an indelible mark on my life. As the men in my group shared their inner struggles, it helped me to open up about my own. Their good example provided me the encouragement to talk about the struggles I faced daily. The step study group was a safe place to be. All that was said remained within the walls of the meeting room.

As the step study progressed, the spiritual blessing was so apparent. A bond of trust grew amongst the men, and we began to relate to each other as brothers in Christ. As individuals we began to have breakthroughs in areas we had been stuck in for years.

I continued to meet with Ron every Tuesday, and he provided much support as the process became difficult. He helped me deal with the issues that surfaced. I worked hard, and each week Ron and I prayed and asked the Lord to bless our time. He did!

I began to sense so many inner conflicts begin to lessen and the feelings of resentment slowly dissipate. When we got to step 9[16], making amends, I knew it was going to be extremely difficult to forgive my brother Chris for the many things that took place while we were growing up.

With the Lord's help I was able to write to my brother and ask for his forgiveness. This was a huge step! I never thought that this area could be changed, but with God's help, it did! I

---

15 Step 4: Make a searching and fearless moral inventory of ourselves.
16 Step 9: Make direct amends to such people whenever possible, except when to do so would injure them or others.

thank the Lord for working through Celebrate Recovery and the men's step study group.

I encourage anyone here to consider signing up for a step study group. The level of commitment required is significant, but the reward is worth it.

Prayer: Thank you, Lord, for each person here. Each person represents a miracle in process. As we walk down the road to recovery, there are many difficulties; however, receiving encouragement from others is a wonderful blessing. One day the road will come to an end and the day of completion will arrive. Our destination will be reached, the Lord Jesus Christ. Amen. Thank you for letting me share.

Eye has not seen, nor ear heard,
Nor have entered into the heart of man
The things which God has prepared for
those who love Him.

1 Corinthians 2:9 (New King James Version)

Miracle after Miracle

Edd Breeden

I love being the pastor at Bonny Doon Church. In early 2019 the previous pastor, a friend of mine, John Burke, suffered a severe heart attack and was compelled to step down as the pastor. The office overseeing Presbyterian churches in this area asked me to come up to help out the church. It did not take long before the board of the church asked me to stay, and I am glad I did.

What do I like so much about the Bonny Doon Church? I love the people and their desire to work together to help Bonny Doon be a better place. I love the variety of ages in the church— from newborns to grandparents. I love the enthusiastic singing on Sunday mornings. And I love the hunger of the people to learn about what the Bible has to say.

You might think the Bible is an old book, full of contradictions and containing many rules of what not to do. That is the way Christianity is often portrayed, but that is not what my learning and experience have taught me. I came to believe in Jesus Christ when I was in college, at the same time I was falling in love with my now wife of 52 years. A miraculous moment drastically changed the course of my life from restaurant design to becoming a pastor.

My wife and I were attending church in Santa Barbara in January of 1970 when I experienced this miraculous moment. I was finishing my last classes as a mathematics major at the University of California in Santa Barbara and was working in a job I thought would be my career path for the whole of my life. That Sunday morning in January, we sat upstairs in the balcony of the church along with the other college students and some high-schoolers. What happened during that hour was to change my thinking completely. It had nothing to do with the sermon or the music, and I did not see anything written on the walls or even hear a voice from heaven. Actually, I don't remember anything happening until I stood up at the end of the service. I turned to my wife and said, "I am going to seminary, I am going to be a pastor." And she said, "Yeah, I know."

We had never talked about my being a pastor. I was quite comfortable with my career. If you had asked me before that church service if I would ever consider being a pastor, I would have quickly told you, "No." Nothing in my life was pointing in that direction, but when the service was over, I knew I had no other life before me than being a pastor.

That day began my journey to grad school and beyond. I had to overcome the hurdle of finishing college first. I remember three miracles between that January Sunday morning and the beginning of seminary in the fall of 1970.

My first hurdle was a particular math class I needed to pass to complete my math degree. As I arrived at my last test, I was hoping it would just go away. I didn't like the course, I hadn't studied well, and I was sure I was headed to a below-passing grade that would prevent me from graduating. The test was an open-book exam, and I still didn't feel confident about it at all. I asked Jesus to help me get through this exam and pass the course, "since it was His fault I needed to finish college anyway." The test was passed out and I looked at the problem. I had no idea what the question was or how to go about looking up the best solution. I prayed again and opened my math book. Right in front of me, on the pages of the book, was the exact problem on the test. I examined it carefully to make sure I was not missing something and then filled out the exam paper exactly as in the book. I turned my paper in early and left the class feeling like Jesus had helped me dodge a big bullet. And yes, I passed the class, graduated, and was moving on.

Then came the second hurdle, the draft. It was 1970 and my draft number was 29; I was sure to be drafted. The only hope I had was my marital status, but they were even taking married men near the end of the Vietnam War. The letter came. I was to report for duty in early June of 1970. I wrote a letter to the draft board that basically said, "God has called me to seminary, and you want me to go into the Army. I would rather follow Jesus." I know other people sent more sophisticated letters, but I was worried. Three days before I was scheduled to report, I received a letter from the head of the draft board in Sacramento: "Your draft notice has been indefinitely postponed. You do not need to report."

I also had the hurdle of learning Greek—the language of the New Testament—so I could pass the entrance exam for seminary. The local Bible college in Santa Barbara was offering a summer class in Greek, so I signed up. The class was six weeks long, from 8 in the morning until noon. I dreaded trying to learn a foreign language since my last attempt at Spanish had failed miserably. So I asked Jesus to do my studying for me and teach me this language. I set my alarm for 6:00 a.m. every morning and studied for an hour and a half before class. After six weeks, I went down to Fuller Seminary to take the entrance exam for New Testament Greek. A few days later I received a call from the people in the language department of the school. I expected they had some bad news for me. But they did not have bad news; they had great news. I had passed the exam and with the highest mark of any who had taken the test that year. They offered me the job of teaching second-year Greek to people who wanted to learn more.

Miracle after miracle.

While at seminary pursuing my master's degree, I learned about the languages used by the original authors of the Bible. Since leaving grad school I have heard many people question the accuracy of the words of the Bible and criticize the book as full of contradictions and errors. But I have found that nothing has changed about the Bible in the last 2,000 years except that many new translations have been printed. The translators do not change the actual words of the Bible, they just adjust the word order a little and provide for the readers a clearer understanding of the meaning of the text. The text of the Bible—from the Old Testament Hebrew to the New Testament Greek—has not changed at all in over 2,000 years. Every time an archaeologist finds a new (actually, an old) copy of some part of the Bible, and they compare it to what they already have, they find no discrepancies, just a few editorial adjustments.

So, why do people think the Bible has been changed over the years and is not the same as it was? I think it is because different people have translated the Greek and Hebrew texts using modern vocabulary. Most people today do not want to listen to movies and TV shows and podcasts in the language of Shakespeare's England. Actually, some of the younger generation don't even want to read with the vocabulary of books I read in high school. There are new words and new idioms that describe things differently in every generation. Changes in words and idioms create the only differences between the many translations of the Bible over the last 2,000 years.

Why is the Bible so important to me? First of all, it has been around for 2,000 years. At one point in my life, I thought it was the only old book in history. I have since learned that I was wrong. Many books were written before the books of the Bible were compiled into its current form.

Second, the Bible contains the teachings of Jesus. To me, Jesus is the most significant person in all of history. I remember learning about Jesus from a pastor in Santa Barbara in the 1960's, while we were preparing to teach some 9th and 10th grade students at a summer camp. He suggested that Jesus was a potential stumbling block for people. Many people think of Jesus as a good teacher, ranked among the most influential people in the history of the world. But think about this for a moment. Not only was He a wonderful teacher, with great ideas that many people want to put into practice, He also claimed to be God. Some say His disciples added that to the Bible after His death, but I have trouble seeing how they could do that. If Jesus claimed to be God when He was not, He was crazy. Either He was a good teacher *and* God, or He was a crazy man claiming to be God and having a few good things to say. I have come to the conclusion that Jesus *was* God and had all the right things to teach us.

Third, the Bible was written by a wide variety of people, from shepherds to fishermen and even some kings. Different parts of the Bible were penned from as early as 800 BC to as late as AD 80; that is a lot of generations. But the story is consistent.

Fourth, I have found tremendous benefits from reading, studying, teaching, and applying the truths of this book. The more I choose to participate in the teachings of Jesus as recorded in the Bible, the more benefits I see in my life. The more I teach others to live by the things Jesus taught, the more I love doing what I do, and I see benefits in their lives as well.

I believe Jesus to be the Messiah for all people, and I have a desire to help others understand why. I love to talk about Jesus and the teachings in the Bible. I love to interact with people who don't see things the way I do. I love to help people who are struggling with spiritual questions. And, I love doing all that in Bonny Doon.

The journey I began back in 1970 took me back to school when I never really liked school and barely passed college. My walk with Jesus caused me to spend four years at seminary in Pasadena, where I not only learned Greek and Hebrew but became a teaching assistant in both languages. After seminary, my family moved to Minnesota, back to California, and then to the coastal region. Living in Scotts Valley brought me to Bonny Doon. What a wonderful journey we have had!

Along the way, I picked up the joy of writing and even started a small business doing taxes for people who need financial help. All in all, it has been a fabulous ride, following where Jesus has led and seeing Him touch the lives of people wherever I have been. I just love helping others.[17]

For we are His workmanship, created in Christ Jesus for good works, which God prepared beforehand so that we would walk in them.

Ephesians 2:10 (NASB)

---

17 If you want to know more about Edd Breeden, see his autobiography *The Drunken Preacher: My Life as a Servant of Jesus,* which is available on Amazon.

Grief and God

Barbara Louv (2017)

"What an awful way to run the universe, God. . . . You let couples love each other for 50 years, and then You take one away causing immense grief to the partner." That was my angry statement to the God of my life when I lost my beloved Ted.

The bottom had fallen out of my life. Gone was the person sharing my joys and sorrows. Gone was the person with whom I shared my everyday experiences. No one to eat meals with. No one to come home to. . . . Empty loneliness greeted me each day.

God had blessed my life with loving parents, educational opportunities, and teaching work that was satisfying. I had healthy children whom I cherished, and I had loved serving others in obedience to God's inspiration. Most of all, I had a wonderful husband who was my best friend.

God had always been my refuge in times of trouble. Where was He now in this experience? I knew the Bible verses in which Paul said that God's power is made perfect in our weakness. His grace is sufficient (2 Corinthians 12:9).

Another says, "For I, the LORD your God, hold your right hand; it is I who say to you, 'Fear not, I will help you.'" Isaiah 41:13 (Revised Standard Version). "I will never fail you nor forsake you." Hebrews 13:5b (RSV).

The Bible is filled with promises of God's presence and concern for us. How could I access these promises of God's? How could I get to a state of peace without my beloved husband beside me?

Then I wondered: Had I already experienced God's infinite Love in this grief? Think back! Wasn't God with me in the small miraculous happenings just after Ted died? Some people might call them coincidences, but I knew in my heart they were gifts from God, and perhaps even Ted.

Only God could have known the experiences of my life. Who knew of the humorous book Ted had given me when we were dating 58 years ago? During the first week of my grief, that book, which I had forgotten in a closet, fell into my hands and brought me out of the depths of my sorrow with laughter! . . . and added to my memory of happier times.

Who sent me to our attic to easily retrieve the soothing love letters we had sent each other in college? I read them and felt renewed.

Who cleared my mind so I could put together a memorial service and make important decisions for the future?

Who prepared the way for Ted to die of cancer before the devastating effects of late Parkinson's disease could torture him?

Who but God has guided my life to this day and provided friends and wonderful, supportive children?

There were messages from God through friends which meant so much, like this one:

"I believe in my heart of hearts that extra love and grace are being sent to you. I believe that your husband's presence will be there to support you through the years to come in ways you cannot yet know. And I believe you will find a way to carry on and smile again."

I haven't felt fearful. I have felt secure. God has been holding my hand this entire time! How will I respond to Him, my Savior and God? I can choose to become bitter and hopeless, and spread misery to all around me. Or, I can choose to follow some healing advice of the Bible.

I searched for that advice, and I found it in many verses:[18]

Philippians 4:6-7 (Revised Standard Version) "Have no anxiety about anything, but in everything by prayer and supplication *with thanksgiving* let your requests be made known to God. And the peace of God, which passes all understanding, will keep your hearts and your minds in Christ Jesus."

Colossians 2:7 "rooted and built up in him . . . abounding in *thanksgiving*."

Colossians 4:2 "Continue steadfastly in prayer, being watchful in it with *thanksgiving;*"

Ephesians 5:20 "always and for everything giving *thanks* in the name of our Lord Jesus Christ to God the Father."

1Thessalonians 5:16-18 "Rejoice always, pray constantly, give *thanks* in all circumstances. . . ."

From the writings of Sarah Young in *Jesus Calling*[19] I read: "As soon as your mind gets snagged on a difficulty, bring it to Me [God] with thanksgiving. The very act of thanking Me releases your mind from its negative focus. As you turn your attention to Me, the problem fades in significance and loses its power to trip you up."

I made a list of things for which I was thankful. It was a very long list, thanking God for everything from my daily routine chores to the very obvious material blessings of my life. I

---

18 Italics added for emphasis.
19 *Jesus Calling: Enjoying Peace in His Presence,* by Sarah Young, copyright 2004 by Sarah Young, page 138.

thanked God for the person who fixed my mailbox and the people around me who gave and needed compassion. I thanked God for my comfortable home in a peaceful nation. Most importantly, I thanked God for the many years of a good marriage to a wonderful man. I reread the list during prayer time to open my heart and mind to the loving presence of God in my life.

God was with me all along. I needed to renew my heart with daily thankfulness to remind me of His love and care.

God is with you. We are His children; He loves us. We are forever in His care . . . even into Eternity.

And the peace of God, which passes all understanding, will keep your hearts and your minds in Christ Jesus.

Philippians 4:7 (RSV)

". . . loss is made endurable by Love
And it is Love that will echo through eternity." [20]

---

20 From *The Midwife: A Memoir of Birth, Joy, and Hard Times* by Jennifer Worth, copyright 2002 by Jennifer Worth, republished by Penguin Books in 2009.

Late Fragment by Raymond Carver[21]

And did you get what
you wanted from this life, even so?
I did.
And what did you want?
To call myself beloved, to feel myself
beloved on the earth.

Journey Home   Author unknown

There's a path that leads to a turn in the road,
And we each must travel there,
Where the Father waits to take us home
To the shelter of His care,
Where happiness and peace and joy
Replace the tears and pain,
And our loved ones rest in the arms of God,
To sweetly live again.

---

21 "Late Fragment" by Raymond Carver, from *A New Path to the Waterfall*, Atlantic Monthly Press, 1989.

Every one to whom much is given, of him
will much be required. . . .

Luke 12:48b (RSV)

A Blessed Life

Barbara Louv (2020)

War can shape a child's developing personality, even though that child is thousands of miles away from the battlefield. Wars have produced prejudices and misgivings between people for thousands of generations. Children are influenced by the prejudices or love around them.

I was born in the United States during World War II to German/Austrian parents. My Mama and Papa were happy and proud to be naturalized American citizens who had come through Ellis Island several years before the conflict. Some of their neighbors were not so happy to have them in the neighborhood during the war.

At home, I was surrounded and protected by my parents' unconditional love. But in 1943 they sent me to public school kindergarten, and I learned about prejudice firsthand from my classmates and teachers. Perhaps it was at that time that I also learned to feel more comfortable away from the spotlight and in the background. Little boys taunting me about my German heritage were to be avoided.

Both of my parents had been brought up Catholic, but had not attended a Catholic church in America. When we moved close to a church in another town, Mama said we were going to attend that church because the building had a cross on it. Within that Presbyterian church the family found loving acceptance by many people. I attended Sunday school and once was sent to the church's summer camp on a scholarship.

When I was about 14, I heard a girl witnessing to her faith in God on the radio. I was hungry for the joy she talked about, and gave my life to Christ then and there. God heard me and came into my life in a new way. I could feel the change, mostly in my attitude. Forgiveness now ruled.

To summarize my life since that time so many years ago would take too many chapters. Suffice it to say, God has blessed me with a life full of contentment, good challenges, joy in serving others, and wonder in His forgiveness of my shortcomings. Of course, my life has not been without problems. Without those, I wouldn't have grown. I handle all of my problems better when I first invite God to be with me in my decision making. That's a lesson I sometimes forget.

I am 81 now and still growing!

May God bless your life with joy, peace, and hope.

The Beautiful Ways of God
or
God Uses All Things

Petra Schultz

Barbara: Today is July 29, 2019, and I am at Petra's house up in Bonny Doon to interview her about her experiences with the Jehovah's Witnesses. Petra, when did you first meet up with the Jehovah's Witnesses?

Petra: It was in the summer of 1984. My twins were just born. They were premature and in the hospital, and I was home alone, missing them. We were living in a remote area at the time. People didn't come to visit me because we were so far away. I was really depressed and recovering from a Cesarean section, and I was lonely because the babies were in the hospital. When a couple of women showed up at my door, I thought to myself, 'Oh, a couple of women. We'll have some tea and cookies and talk about the Bible. How perfect is that!' So it was all very nice and sweet, and the women talked about things that sounded interesting, like living forever.

The only Bible I had in the house at that time was a King James Bible that I had received from the Presbyterian church when I was about nine, so I was using that when the women came the first couple of times. Then they said, "Maybe you should have a newer Bible, a more updated English version." I had no idea about Bibles or translations. I never went to church except when I was a kid a few times. I didn't grow up in a Christian home, really. My Mom just sent us to Sunday school a few times, so I was very ignorant about what the scripture says about Christ. It was nice having these women come by, and I ended up getting one of their Bibles called the *New World Translation*. They showed me a couple of passages that made it seem like the English was more up to date, and it was only four dollars, so I got a new Bible.

I started studying with them, and one thing led to another. I began reading the *Watchtower* and *Awake!* magazines, and finally my baby boys came home from the hospital. The ladies came about once a week or every other week to have a little Bible study and talk about this book called *You Can Live Forever in Paradise on Earth*. I believed everything they said because I had nothing to reference it to.

After a while I started going to the Kingdom Hall on Sunday, and there was a *Watchtower* study after the service. They started encouraging me to go to other Bible studies. There was a theocratic study on Thursday night, and a new book study of whatever new book Watchtower had published. So that was like four meetings a week. Then they said, "You really should come to *all* the meetings." There were five meetings a week that I could have gone to, and this is how these sisters explained it: They said it was kind of like falling over a cliff, and you were hanging on for your life to a branch with only one hand. That one hand has five fingers. Five fingers are like five meetings. Now, if you only go to four meetings, you are hanging on to your life with only four fingers, and if you only go to two meetings, you aren't going to have much of a grip. You are not going to make it into the system of things because you are only going to two meetings. That made me feel afraid. I felt that I really should go to all those meetings.

My husband didn't know much about Christianity, so he thought it sounded okay, you know, reading about the Bible. It sounds like a clean activity. So I went. One of the books was called *Creation*, and I believe in creation, so there was nothing wrong with *that* book.

Barbara: When did you first start noticing that something was wrong?

Petra: Good question. Okay, so I have twins and when they were babies they were a lot of work to take care of, so I couldn't go to all the meetings. I actually stopped going when we moved up to Bonny Doon and started building a house. So the sisters came up and approached me here. I didn't tell them I was quitting or anything; I just couldn't go, so they came up here. They wanted me to do service going door to door. My husband was firmly against this. He said, "You're not going to do that. Don't bother people door to door." I was willing to stand on a corner, do phone service, anything, but my husband was really against me going door to door. So these sisters encouraged me. They said, "This is what you do. When your husband goes off to work, you go door to door. Come home before he gets home from work, and he will never know." I thought, 'That sounds sneaky. That doesn't sound right.' That was the first thing that didn't seem right to me.

I was also learning through the *Watchtower* studies that all other Christian churches in the world were under the influence of Satan. They taught me that I shouldn't go to church, and if any Christian literature came to my house through the mail, I was not supposed to look at it. They said, "Don't be curious. Don't look at it. Throw it in the garbage. Just throw it in the garbage. Don't pay any attention to it because you are opening up a window to Satan." I did what they said. I was so brainwashed because of everything I was reading and studying. I was reading the *Watchtower* and *Awake!*, their Bible, their books. Everything was printed by the Watchtower Society. Even their Greek interlinear translation was printed by the Watchtower Society, so it was all very biased towards their religion. That was the beginning of things going wrong.

One year my husband brought home a Christmas tree and I wouldn't decorate it. It just leaned against the wall dying. I don't remember what I said about that tree, but I must have said something about Grandma and Grandpa and that Christmas trees are evil. The kids were starting to grow up. They were about four at this time, so the boys told my husband that I had said that Grandma and Grandpa were evil because they had a Christmas tree. My husband said, "That does it. You are not calling my Mom and Dad evil."

After that he didn't want those women to come into our house any more, but I started to study with them secretly. We would meet in the car, across from the firehouse, to do our little study together. I wasn't going to the meetings, though, because that would be on a Sunday, and I didn't want my husband to find out. The sisters at the Kingdom Hall would rather have me be divorced from my husband. That would be okay with them because he wasn't a believer. It was also okay with them to be sneaky. It wasn't good.

⁂

My husband was worried. He felt that he needed to do something about this situation, so he got a Bible. He was at work when someone noticed that he had a Bible on the dashboard of his truck.

They said, "Hey, John, so you are reading the Bible?"

And he said, "Well, not really. I don't know anything about the Bible. My wife is studying with the Jehovah's Witnesses and I don't know what to do. She is learning all this crazy stuff."

"I tell you what," this person said, "I know what you can do. There is this couple down in San Jose that has a ministry helping people know more about the Jehovah's Witnesses. Schedule a meeting with them, and bring your wife if she is willing to come. Go talk with them."

While that was happening with John, I remember that I wanted to be baptized. I felt really strong. I had been studying and learning for a few years, and I thought I was ready to be baptized. So the sisters said that I needed to talk to one of the brothers at the Kingdom Hall. I guess I must have gone to one of the meetings. Anyway, I remember talking to the brothers at the Kingdom Hall after a meeting, and I told them I wanted to be baptized.

They said, "Well, you have to go door to door."

"But that is something my husband is strongly against," I answered.

"Well, you have to do that to prove yourself to Jehovah," they said.

"But I will stand on the corner; I will witness to people; I will talk to people everywhere I go, and hand out *Watchtowers*."

"You really have to go door to door," they insisted.

"There is a scripture in the Bible about Philip and the Ethiopian," I said. "The Ethiopian saw a body of water and said, 'What prevents me from being baptized?'[22] *He* was baptized. *He* didn't go door to door."

---

22 Acts 8:36 (New American Standard Bible)

At this, all the brothers could do was shrug their shoulders, so I left. I never was baptized. But this made me start to question things—you know—that passage about Philip didn't agree with their teaching. Even in *their* Bible it didn't agree. How could they argue?

My husband did arrange a meeting with this couple in San Jose, so I went. I was feeling so prepared. I had been reading my books, and I had lots of scriptures memorized. I was pretty reluctant, but I did go. So we went, and it was around Christmas time. They had lots of Christmas lights up and a Christmas tree, and I thought, 'Oh my gosh! I am in the house of Satan!' I was gritting my teeth, and I said to myself, 'I will just sit through this.'

This couple showed me copies of the *Watchtower* from the early 1900's, from the 1920's, and from 1975. They were about previous predictions of the end of time—telling people they would live forever. But the world didn't end in 1925, and the world didn't end in 1975, so these were false predictions. The Bible says in Deuteronomy that if a prophet's predictions do not happen, then they are not from God. *So,* the governing body and the Watchtower Society are *not* divine. God does not speak through them because He wouldn't speak lies. They gave both John and me booklets with all these copies of old *Watchtowers* and *Awake!* and a lot of other materials about inaccuracies in their Greek interlinear translation. So we took these home with us.

The sisters knew I was going to go to this meeting. They came to me, and said,

"How did the meeting go?"

"Well, they gave me this book," I said.

"Oh my gosh, you should burn that!"

"Yeah, you are right," I replied.

So I put it in the wood stove and burned it. But they didn't know that John had a copy too (laughter), and I secretly kept that from them. I wanted to appease them, so I burned my copy, but I was very reluctant. I didn't know what the truth *was* anymore, so I didn't believe these sisters. I was in—this fog. When they left, I felt that I just wanted to know the truth, so I prayed to God, "I just want to know the truth."

Barbara: What happened after that?

Petra: I stopped going to the Kingdom Hall. For about two weeks I sat at my kitchen table with different translations of the Bible I had borrowed, and a *Strong's Concordance*. I just kept looking up scriptures and comparing all the different versions. I discovered that in the Jehovah's Witness Bible, the *New World Translation*, the name "Jehovah" isn't there at all. They have added words to make things sound different.

For example, when the Bible says that everything was created *through* Christ, they put in brackets the word *other*—all [other] things were created through Christ—meaning that Christ was also created. These little changes make you believe really different things. In the book of Hebrews it says that we are not supposed to worship angels. Well, they believe that Jesus is Michael the Archangel, but they say that people didn't worship him, they did "obeisance" to him. So they change words. Instead of "worship" they say "obeisance." They change things to make it seem so different.

I didn't really know what to do with myself. I still loved God, and I wanted to know more. Then I saw in the *Battle Mountain News*[23] (this is huge, God answered my prayer!) that there was a women's Bible study in Sherry McDermott's home. (This was around 1988.) I felt safe. It wasn't in a church. It was in someone's home, so I went. That is where I met these most wonderful women—Sherry McDermott, Marge Roussopoulos, Helen Robb, Marion Wahl, and others. I met so many wonderful women. I told Sherry where I was coming from and she said, "Oh my goodness, God loves you so much!" and I said, "Yeah, He does."

Soon after that I was at home and the propane guy was delivering propane. I thought, 'Oh boy, I have to go talk to this person,' because every time he came I would give him the *Watchtower* and *Awake!* magazines. I went down to him and said, "I just want to apologize for giving you those magazines." But after I apologized, he told me that he had been praying for me, and he asked if I had received Jesus. I said, "No," so he suggested that we pray together. I prayed with him and accepted Jesus that day.

Barbara: Wow! That is amazing.

Petra: Yeah. That was pretty cool. God uses mysterious ways for people to get saved.

So where were we? Oh, yes. I went to the Bonny Doon Bible study for years, but I wasn't ready to go to a church at first, not until maybe the second year. I wondered where the other women went to church, and all these women went to different churches. I thought, 'Why would people go to different

---

23 A monthly newsletter for the Bonny Doon community.

churches?' We were taught by the Jehovah's Witnesses that all these denominations were an indication of disorder. But God was the God of order, not disorder. The Jehovah's Witnesses had an explanation for everything.

Sherry went to University Baptist Church, with pastor Marv Webster, and I thought, 'I am going to go there.' So I went there for a little while, and then I decided to get baptized. I remember the day I was baptized. I was in the back room getting my gown on, and there were a few girls there from the university. They were all laughing and giggling, and I was crying and crying. My husband and the boys were there. The boys were still little. They were in the front seat watching me get baptized. I still have my little confirmation of baptism letter.

My life changed. I really believe that it changed then. I don't know if I was filled with the Holy Spirit then, but my life changed. God was speaking to me in a different way. I could hear His voice. He was telling me who I am, and what I am. It was like, 'Oh, I didn't realize I did that,' and 'Oh, I didn't realize I thought that.' It is interesting. I don't know how to explain it. I saw myself differently through the Holy Spirit, and things started changing in my life.

Then one day I decided to check out the Bonny Doon Church. One of the other women from the Bible study went there. There were only about 10 people when I first came, and they were looking for a pastor. That was when Pastor John Burke came on board. I have been at Bonny Doon Church ever since, although I moved away to Canada for a little while and came back. Bonny Doon Church has been a solid rock.

I still had all this false doctrine floating around in my head, and I didn't know what to do about it. Santa Cruz Bible Church had an evening when some ex-Jehovah's Witnesses came to share. I was so drawn to hear other people's stories. I couldn't get enough of it. I read books about the differences between Mormonism and Jehovah's Witnesses. I wanted confirmation that, 'Yeah, they *are* brain-washers. They are a false religion.' I needed confirmation of that all the time.

Jumping ahead 10 years, we moved to Canada. My first priority was finding a new church up there. My husband didn't go to church, but he encouraged me. So that was good. We just looked through the yellow pages. I didn't know how to look for a church. We found the Evangelical South Shore Church. It was a nice church about twice the size of Bonny Doon Church, and I felt right at home there. The first time I attended a service, there was a woman sitting in front of me. Her name was Linda, and she became my awesome friend.

One of the great things that happened while I was at that church was that I went to an Alpha course.[24] I learned a lot about the fundamental beliefs of Christianity from the Alpha course, and that was very important and helpful to me. The other thing I was exposed to there was The Wordless Book.[25] This is a simple book of wordless colored pages used for explaining the gospel to children. The simple truths that I learned there cleared my head of a lot of the Jehovah's Witnesses' teachings. It really helped me. It was profound for me because I had to learn everything all over again like a child.

_____

24 See www.alpha.org The Alpha course is an 11-week course that freely explores the fundamental beliefs of the Christian faith.

25 See https://www.letthelittlechildrencome.com/child-evangelism-resources/ wordless-book-share-the-gospel The Wordless Book uses basic colors to explain the gospel. Gold represents heaven where everything is perfect. Black is the sin in our hearts, which cannot enter heaven, or heaven would no longer be perfect. Red is the blood of Jesus, who died to take away the punishment for our sins. White is how our hearts can be if we accept Jesus' gift of forgiveness and salvation. Green represents our new life in Christ as we grow in our faith.

We were in Canada for about three and a half years. When I moved back to Bonny Doon and started going to the Bonny Doon Church again, Sue Cannon, Denby Adamson, and I started an Alpha course here in Bonny Doon. It was highly successful and was an encouragement and blessing to our church members.

What I keep learning over the years is how important it is to trust God and be thankful. There is always something to be thankful for even during a struggling time or a crisis. You can still be thankful for so many things. God has been watching over me. I am thankful that God took me out of the Jehovah's Witnesses. I don't hate them. I don't hate anyone, but I am concerned about the governing body of the Jehovah's Witnesses and what they teach. I don't even know what they are teaching now.

And we know that God causes all things
to work together for good to those who love
God, to those who are called according to
His purpose.

Romans 8:28 (NASB)

Now to Him who is able to do exceedingly abundantly above all that we ask or think, according to the power that works in us, to Him be glory in the church by Christ Jesus to all generations, forever and ever. Amen.

Ephesians 3:20-21 (New King James Version)

God Hears

Petra Schultz

When I was 20, I had been working hard at a job in a plastic mold injection factory, building parts for Ford Ranger pickups. One Sunday afternoon at work, I was eating my lunch outside by myself on the grass, and out of the blue I said to God, "There has got to be something better than this." That was all. I didn't dwell on it, and I didn't try to change my life.

But then I got sick.

I developed a lung infection due to the dirty working conditions caused by the plastic fumes, and the doctor said I had to quit my job if I wanted to get well. God knew that I would never have quit that job unless something drastic happened, but He also knew what He wanted to do with my future even when I had no idea.

About 10 years later I was sitting in a Bible study, and I remembered the prayer I had prayed years earlier. I was dumbfounded, because during those 10 years my life had turned around 180 degrees, and I hadn't even realized it. I was now married to a wonderful man, had two wonderful sons, and was building a house in Bonny Doon. I had become a Christian, and was going to church and Bible studies. My life had become what Jesus calls "abundant."

I thanked God, and I cried and cried, because I knew that the Lord had heard me, had been merciful to me, and had blessed me beyond anything I ever imagined.

Anxiety in the heart of man causes depression,
But a good word makes it glad.

Proverbs 12:25 (New King James Version)

God Laughs

Petra Schultz

I see my Father in heaven in all that He has made, especially in springtime when the trees are in blossom, flowers are everywhere, and gentle rain is falling from the redwoods. I realize that God made many things simply to be beautiful, for His pleasure and for us to enjoy.

One day, God gave me a new insight into His great and loving personality. Early that morning I was feeling kind of down, so I went outside to get the mail and feed the chickens, then I wandered through the orchard and up to a blooming plum tree. I was admiring the blossoms of the tree, and I was still sad for no particular reason. I was thanking God for all the beauty of the garden and trees, and I said I was sorry, but I didn't know why I was feeling sad. I went close to a plum blossom and breathed in deeply, and the blossom went right up my nose. It surprised me. I snorted and laughed and smiled and looked up to heaven, and I knew God was smiling at me. I laughed about that all day.

A Reflection[26]

John Burke

As we grow older (or perhaps younger in spirit),
As we grow older and the sand of time rushes through the
      hourglass,
As we grow older our children seem younger and younger,
As we grow older the eternal majesty of God grows brighter,
As we grow older.

So let us dance the glorious dance of faith and joy,
Let us dance in our hearts and minds the dance of grateful
      redemption,
Let us dance the dance of acceptance—and curtsy to Jesus,
Let us lift up our voice in praise as the hours pass,
For He who holds the worlds in His hands holds our hands also.
Let us dance gravely and solemnly with our Creator,
For He has invited us to the everlasting dance.

---

26 John was inspired by listening to a performance of Beethoven's Mass in C.

Life Narrative

John Burke

When I was seven years old, my parents moved to Bolinas, California, a small fishing and tourist village. My father was in seminary in San Francisco, and at the same time he was the student-appointed pastor of the Bolinas Presbyterian church. I spent my time when not in school going down to the ocean to hunt delicious white clams, walk the beach, and sometimes watch storm waves crash into a 7-foot-high concrete bulkhead alongside the ocean. Sometimes I climbed up the 75-foot-high sandstone cliffs that guarded the ocean and were bordered by ice plant.

One day after going down to the beach to watch big storm waves, I got too close to the edge of the bulkhead and slipped on the green algae—right into the churning, frothy green seawater 6 feet below. In God's providence the storm waves paused for several moments, and a cross current along the face of the bulkhead dragged me about 75 feet and washed me up on the other side. I staggered out of the water—cold, wet, and glad to be alive. I knew that God had saved me.

That same year the Reverend Billy Graham held an evangelistic crusade at the Cow Palace in San Francisco. My mother was a crusade counselor and began to be concerned about her family members, including her middle son, myself. One day she took me aside and asked if I would like to go to heaven instead of hell, and if so would I ask Jesus into my heart to forgive my sins. The prospect of going to hell scared me a lot, and I quickly prayed to accept Jesus in my heart.

We continued to live in Bolinas for another couple of years. I free-climbed the tall sandstone cliffs along the ocean.

Many times I was saved from falling by grabbing the ice plant stringers on the edges of the cliffs. God was watching out for my life.

After my father completed his pastoral seminary studies, we moved to Felton, California, a small town nestled in the Santa Cruz mountains. During the next seven years I went to school and also got an after-school gardening job to save money for college. I was a quiet boy who read novels. Church and God began to recede in importance, although I still had big questions about my life.

In my junior year of high school we moved again—this time to Bisbee, Arizona. I felt out of place in my new school, so I graduated in the middle of my senior year and went with my older brother to work in a lumber mill in Montana. That fall I enrolled in Northern Arizona University in Flagstaff and began a pre-med degree. I attended the campus Christian fellowship a couple of times, but soon dropped out. I had became a practical agnostic.

During my second year of college, my older brother came to visit and told me about unusual events happening in San Francisco—that year would become known as the "Summer of Love." I left college and went to Haight-Ashbury[27] with my brother to learn about this new lifestyle. I tried marijuana and LSD, and quickly had neither money nor many possessions.

One day while talking with a woman I had met, we began heatedly arguing about God and Satan. She declared her belief in the devil; for the sake of argument, I took the side of God. During the argument I suddenly had an awakening. I just knew in an instant that God was real, and that I believed in Jesus. Later

---

27 A neighborhood in San Francisco that is known as the birthplace of the hippie counterculture of the 1960's.

that week I went to a Christian coffee house in the "Haight" that also served free lunches. I was couch surfing and didn't have permanent housing. I told some new Christian friends about my experience of finding God, and they said, "Come stay with us at our house." I spent some time with them and then decided to travel to Southern California with a friend. This journey would eventually lead me down to Costa Mesa, where I became part of Pastor Chuck Smith's newly formed Calvary Chapel—at that time a church of about 200. While at Calvary Chapel, I and two friends staffed the first youth house. We invited new converts to join us, and soon there were three houses. Young people were coming to Christ almost every day. I planned to go to Biola College, but before I could start, I was drafted into the U.S. Army at Fort Ord.

At Fort Ord I was chosen to become a medic. My drill sergeant was a Christian who forbade swear words, and also taught our bay of soldiers how to work together, help each other, and be successful soldiers. After 10 weeks of Basic Training, I went to Fort Sam Houston for medic training. Then I was sent to Columbia, South Carolina, and became a hospital corpsman and ambulance driver. At that time I thought about becoming a doctor and helping people through medicine.

After serving for almost two years in the army, I went home to Aztec, New Mexico, and enrolled in Fort Lewis College in Durango, Colorado. During my junior year, I changed my life direction and decided to enter seminary to become a missionary. I was influenced by being part of a very active Christian college group, which grew to 50 or 60 people during my college years.

When I graduated from college I went to Fuller Seminary for three years. My goal was to become a Wycliffe[28] missionary

28 Wycliffe Bible Translators. See https://www.wycliffe.org.

and translate the Bible into an unknown tribal language. After graduating from seminary, I went to the Summer Institute of Linguistics in North Dakota [a Wycliffe partner organization]. Unfortunately, at the end of the summer I was not chosen to go on to any further Wycliffe training. My linguistic verbal skills were only modest, so I was not a good translator candidate. Apparently, I had a poor ear for language.

I spent the next several months working in a hospital as an orderly and became very depressed. I realized that I needed to do full-time ministry rather than orderly hospital work. So that was how my ministerial career began.

* * *

I took a job as a half-time youth pastor on San Juan Island in Washington state. I worked there for a year and a half, but when my father died, I felt like I needed a break from pastoral work and so returned to Santa Cruz County. I worked as a kindergarten teacher for one semester in a Christian school near Watsonville. I had a great time, but eventually ran out of art projects and activities for kindergartners! My next job was in Cupertino at Tymshare, Inc., which served the airline industry's data-processing needs. I stayed for about a year and then transferred to a computer school in San Jose, where I began teaching computer subjects and English. About this time I also began volunteering at New Life Center in Santa Cruz doing pastoral work.

Even though I dated off and on, I had a great need in my life. I didn't have a life partner. One day I got down on my knees and said to God, "Whoever you next bring into my life will be the person I am supposed to marry." About a month later I met Barbara Sutton while she was volunteering as a church secretary in the Santa Cruz Christian and Missionary Alliance Church. After we had been dating for several months, I had a desire to know from God if "she was the one." I directly asked God in prayer, and I heard an audible voice speak one sentence, "Will you support her?" This was confirmation for me, and we were married about four months later—just before Christmas.

My new wife, Barbara, was concerned because I was only working part-time while volunteering at New Life Center as an "Associated Pastor." At this time I heard that the Felton Presbyterian Church needed a youth pastor. I inquired and was accepted as the new youth pastor, a post that I held for about one and a half years, working with Reverend Don Munro. The church eventually had budgetary problems, and I was released from service. About this time I heard from Reverend Dick Dosker, who had been filling in at the Bonny Doon Presbyterian Church, that the church needed a pastor. He wanted to know if I was interested. I was, and my wife and I interviewed with the church session at the Davenport Inn. I was accepted and began as the new pastor on Palm Sunday—with some trepidation—I wasn't sure how the church usually celebrated the Easter season! That year I also began holding an Easter sunrise service at 6:30 a.m. at the church, a celebration which continues to this day. My wife began a Sunday school for our kids. Soon other families came with their children, and the church grew.

During my years pastoring the Bonny Doon Presbyterian Church, I worked in computer software in San Jose part-time. I wrote a book on internet databases along with elder Bob Neilson, which was published by Que Publishing. I also enrolled in Capella University and eventually received a doctorate in clinical psychology. I used the specialized training to counsel substance abusers and church members.

Some special times with God:

March 5, 1985
"Jesus is coming." These words were spoken in my dream and were accompanied by a brilliant, white, startling light—so pure, so holy, I was awed by His glory, His majesty, His truth, and His presence.

May 17, 1988
I dreamed that I was asked to go to a church, and as I walked in, a double processional of figures in white were walking down the aisle toward the front of the church. I heard beautiful praises, and the ceiling of the building was lit with a rosy glow. Suddenly I realized that it was Sunday and it was communion. Jesus was gladly and joyously taking bread and wine to members of the congregation. He seemed so full of joy, so full of life, so full of love, my heart was joyous as I watched this lovely scene and realized that He loved being with each person there. Then I awoke. All was so natural, yet so heightened in spiritual perception.

May 12, 2018
I was praying by myself next to the heater in the Kirk House, and suddenly, although my eyes were closed, I was seated in "a chair of glory." I looked down, and I was suspended in a chair of glory that was holding me up and was maybe 10 inches above the floor on each side of me. It was as if I was encased and surrounded, from my feet to my head, in glory itself—beautiful—and I heard these words, "You will judge the nations." The following words came to mind. "If then you were raised with Christ, seek those

things which are above, where Christ is, sitting at the right hand of God." Colossians 3:1 (New King James Version)

". . . and made us sit together in the heavenly places . . ." Ephesians 2:6 (NKJV)

June 21, 2019
I was asleep at about 4:30 a.m., when I found myself on my face —weeping—at the feet of Jesus. I wept and cried because of my sins. I also realized that He was giving me acceptance and grace, but I kept repenting of my sinfulness in His pure presence. I awoke later and realized He had entered my dream. He was all white—purest white—mighty but not scary. I was completely awed in His presence. When I awoke at 7:13 a.m., I still sensed His presence during my intercession and prayer.

Let Not Your Heart Be Troubled

John Burke

In My Father's House

John Burke

Reflections on My Mother's Life

Barbara Burke

As my mother once said, "This is not a story you would normally hear." What she meant, I think, is that her life story had so many twists and turns that you couldn't make logical sense of it. She felt that it was fragmented, disjointed, and characterized by tragedy and loss—hardly the ingredients for a story anyone would want to hear. Since she couldn't make sense of it herself, she chose not to tell it. She didn't want to write it herself, and she didn't want to be interviewed for a book. Her attitude was, "The past is dead and buried. You don't need to be burdened with these things."

Although I grew up without knowing many of the details of my mother's life, this beautiful quote by Dietrich Bonhoeffer expresses something I always felt was true.

> The important thing today is that we should be able to discern from the fragment of our life how the whole was arranged and planned, and what material it consists of . . . I'm thinking, for example, of the *Art of Fugue*. If our life is but the remotest reflection of such a fragment, if in a short time we accumulate a wealth of themes and weld them together into a pleasing harmony and keep the great counterpoint going all through, when it comes to an untimely conclusion, we can still sing the Grand Chorale, and we will not bemoan the fragmentariness of our life, but rather rejoice in it.[29]

---

29 From a letter to Eberhard Bethge, 21 February 1944. In *Letters and Papers from Prison* by Dietrich Bonhoeffer, copyright 1953, SCM Press, London.

It is with joy that I tell my mother's story, as I know it.

My mother, Kazimiera Anna Komarzanska, later called Katherine,[30] was born on October 1, 1919, in Lvov, Poland. She had a mother, Anna, and father, Jan, whom we know very little about. She also had one younger sister, Jadwiga, who had polio. Katherine often told me that her mother spent a lot of time caring for Jadwiga, which required her to become independent fairly quickly, and also led to her developing a close relationship with her father. (I was happy to know that because I had a close relationship with my father, also.)

After Katherine finished parochial high school in Lvov, she became engaged to a young man from a landowner's family; but before they were able to marry, he and his family had to flee Poland when the policy of agrarianism led to the redistribution of land to the peasants. This was Katherine's first encounter with political forces that would change her life forever. Even though she was brokenhearted, she was able to keep her eye on the future. She enrolled in secretarial school, graduated, and got her first job in a different city in eastern Poland. She must have been quite independent by then, and this was fortunate, since her life was about to take an unexpected turn for the second time.

Soon, my mother met another man, Arnold Ball, whom she fell in love with and married. He was a handsome Jewish actor from Germany who had come to Poland to live. But shortly after their marriage, in 1939, Germany invaded Poland from the west, and weeks later the Soviet Union invaded Poland from the

---

30 Members of the Bonny Doon Church called her Kitty.

east. Katherine and Arnold were deported to Siberia with more than a million other Polish citizens. We don't know much about the two and a half years they lived there. We only know that they had a bit more freedom than other people because Arnold was an actor who was sent out to entertain troops. Katherine clearly did not want to talk about this time in her life, and my brother and I can only imagine some of the difficulties she endured as a prisoner of war.

In 1941, as a result of Hitler's army attacking the Soviet Union, the Soviets joined the Allies, and an agreement was made to release the Polish prisoners and form a Polish army to fight against Hitler. Katherine planned to join the Polish army, and in 1943, with hundreds of thousands of other Polish citizens, she was sent to Tashkent (in what is now Uzbekistan) to receive food, uniforms, and supplies. From there, some of the soldiers, including my mother, were sent out once again, to Iran (previously called Persia). Unfortunately, Arnold had been detained in the Soviet Union. Katherine found out later that he was killed because he was a Jew.

When Katherine arrived in Iran in 1943, she was very ill with typhus and malaria. She was hospitalized for months, and once she was released, it took her almost a year to recover. She told us many times that having suffered loss, deprivation, and sickness, she really wanted to die. She had lost all hope, and this is hardly surprising. At only 24 years of age, she had already lived on three continents, under two dictators, not by choice. She had lost her husband and everyone in her family, and she felt completely alone.

It was then that two Polish refugees, whose names she didn't remember but who had suffered similar experiences, said to her, "Pull yourself up . . . keep living." She said these simple words really helped her.

Life began to improve for Katherine. She said that the six years she lived in Iran were some of the best years of her life. She healed physically and made lasting friendships. Kindness shown by the Iranians toward the Polish refugees brought hope into her world. She told us many times that the sunshine and beaches of the Caspian Sea were like a healing salve to her weary body. Not only did she enjoy the natural environment, food, and people, but she experienced a new sense of freedom.

My mother was a beautiful woman. She met my father—a German, Jewish man who had fled Hitler—in Tehran, the capital of Iran. Franz Sittenfeld was a confirmed bachelor who was swept off his feet by her. He charmed her with fur coats, jewelry, and his great personality! She loved her life in Tehran. She often told us how wonderful and welcoming the Iranian people were. She met and socialized with my father's friends, and slowly made Tehran her home. Franz proposed to her, she accepted, and they were married by a Presbyterian minister in 1949 in the American Embassy in Tehran.[31]

Shortly after their marriage, Katherine and Franz were advised by a confidante to leave Iran. They were told that if they didn't leave Iran then, it would be more difficult for them in the future. The political climate was changing, and the Europeans who had been so welcomed in the past were considered supporters of the Shah. Religious tolerance was also changing. My mother was a Christian raised in the Catholic tradition, and my father was Jewish. They were warned that with the growth of the Islamic movement in Iran, there would be less tolerance of diverse faiths. My parents decided to immigrate to the USA,

---

31 They were both declared stateless, and there was an American Protestant missionary who was willing to marry them.

encouraged by my father's cousin who had settled in Oakland, California, several years before. They came, but like many immigrants they had mixed emotions. Katherine said many times that living in the USA was a blessing, but she often felt that she had her "feet in two cultures."

Over time, my mother embraced her new country and her new life. She put the past behind her. Both she and my father became naturalized citizens, changing their names to Katherine Anne Sutton and Frank Richard Sutton. Katherine learned English, learned how to drive, raised two children, joined the PTA, joined a church, worked in a hospital, and later got her real estate license. By the time I was 17, she had a wide circle of friends, both American and European.

It is not difficult to see that Katherine had tremendous courage. She was also a "people person." She developed a gift of hospitality. She was elegant and gracious, and she served others. She pointed my brother and me toward faith in God by taking us with her to church as young children, and she introduced us to art, music, languages, and cultures. She showed us, by example, how to care for others and be sensitive to their needs. She provided us with the example of how to be faithful to each other and to our friends and families. What stands out to me is that despite each apparent roadblock, she lived out this command of Moses to the people of Israel:

> Today I have given you the choice between life and death, between blessings and curses. Now I call on heaven and earth to witness the choice you make. Oh, that you would choose life, so that you and your descendants might live!

Deuteronomy 30:19 (New Living Translation)

For Katherine to choose life was not just to focus on physical and emotional healing, although at times she had to do that, but also to make choices that would impact her future, her children, grandchildren, and great-grandchildren forever. Moses told his people to listen to God and obey His commandments. This commitment—this choice—had a significant impact on her life and the lives of her family members.

My mother was raised in eastern Poland, in a region which has been described as "very Catholic." She had a deep love and respect for the teachings of the church, and one of the few stories she told me over and over again was how she loved to go to Mass once a week with her father. She received religious instruction in the church and parochial school. We know that for more than two years of her life in Siberia, she had little contact with Christians. Later, among my father's friends in Iran, she socialized with many Jewish people from Europe who had fled Hitler. Speaking about God among these Jewish friends was certainly possible, but judging by my father's turn toward agnosticism, it may not have been appreciated. There were many Jewish people who were so traumatized by what they knew Hitler was doing to the Jews in Europe, that they completely abandoned their faith, concluding that God had failed them.

Despite this, my mother's faith did not die. Her faith in God was real, and she believed that it was because of God's sovereignty that she had survived the first quarter of her life. One of her memories was that an aunt had always prayed for her. As soon as she came to America and was settled in Oakland, California, she found a small Christian church in the neighborhood and began attending. My father, a Jewish agnostic who considered himself liberal and tolerant in his views about religion, did not try to stop or dissuade her from dressing up on

Sunday and taking my brother and me to church. (She walked there, and in high heels, by the way!) He stayed home, drank coffee, and read the Sunday paper. Katherine wanted to expose her children to faith in God, and she longed for a place where she could pray and worship again. Although she noticed the cultural differences between this small Protestant church and her own Catholic church in Poland, she put them aside. She was seeking God, not a certain way of worshiping Him.

At this small Presbyterian church in Oakland, Katherine was introduced to Paul and Elizabeth Yates, immigrants from Poland (Paul) and Germany (Elizabeth). They had immigrated a year after my parents and had similar life experiences as my mother and father. Paul, raised in the Jewish faith, had become a follower of Jesus and now called himself a Hebrew Christian (or Messianic Jew). Elizabeth was Catholic, like my mother. Katherine was immediately drawn toward this couple, and vice versa. They began coming to our home and soon became friends with my father. They were gracious and accepting, and of course could relate to my parents' backgrounds. My father accepted their invitation to church and began visiting the Yates' home, where the name of Yeshua (Jesus) was always spoken and honored.

When I was about nine years old, my father publicly professed his belief in Jesus Christ as the Messiah and was baptized. In a room full of people, he testified, "I was blind, but now I can see." He also declared his need for forgiveness from sin, which, for him, was a beautiful move towards humility. Discipled by Paul Yates as well as by the pastor of our neighborhood church in Oakland, my father grew in his new faith. Because of this, my brother and I were raised in a home where Jesus Christ was honored and the Bible (both the Old and

New Testament) was read. We are eternally grateful for the courage and foresight my mother and father had in raising us this way and remaining true to what they believed. Their commitment to faith served as the example on which my brother and I have built our lives.

My father retired in 1974, and he and my mother moved to a house in Mount Hermon, near Santa Cruz. Then as happens in life, a few years later tragedy struck once again. In 1977, without any forewarning, my father died of a massive heart attack. At the age of 57, my mother became a widow for the second time. It took two long years of grieving before she set her heart and mind toward living again. This time she was filled with the understanding that "a life of giving is a life worth living," so she sought opportunities to serve others who were facing the challenges and struggles of life. She volunteered at the local hospital emergency room and later took a paid position with Meals on Wheels. She worked passionately, delivering meals to homebound residents of Santa Cruz County until she finally retired at age 94.

My mother's story does not have a conclusion. She passed away when she was 99 years old, six months shy of her 100th birthday. She is with God, at peace, in her eternal home. I no longer need to know the details of her life. As Bonhoeffer said so beautifully, I rejoice that the fragments of her life produced a wealth of themes, which were welded together into a pleasing harmony, by a compassionate and loving God. She is now singing the Grand Chorale!

I Am a Christian

Bob Hughes

I am a Christian. Had you heard me speak this, rather than reading it, there would not have been a tone of bravado or bragging, but a small emphasis on the word "Christian." I would not have shouted, "I AM A CHRISTIAN!" Nor would I have said, "I am a Christian?" The words, "I am a Christian" should be said with humility, but with a positive attitude.

I don't know when I became a believer in God and Jesus; the feeling gradually became stronger as the years passed. I do remember a specific incident. I was on an airplane for a business trip sometime in the mid-1980's. As the pilot was beginning the take-off procedures, I prayed to God that the flight would be uneventful. Instantly, I heard in my head, loud and clear, "So be it my son." In later air travel, I never felt the need for prayer on that subject again.

My Christian beliefs are plain and simple. I believe that God is my heavenly Father and that He created all things and continues to do so. He is the ruler of Heaven and Earth. God loves each of us and cares for us. He guides us through life, but, yes, does give us free will. What we do with that free will determines our final judgment call from God. I fully accept Jesus, God's only begotten Son, as my Savior, my Redeemer, my Healer, and my Friend.

I am not a Bible reader, but I greatly enjoy listening to a preacher who is. Hearing the words of Jesus and learning His teachings gives me a strength I cannot describe.

I am a piano player and have been playing God's hymns for 65 years. Worshiping through music is important to me. Playing hymns on the church's piano before the Sunday service gives me a strong link to both God and Jesus, as does playing them at home. I use Christian music to change moods, to relax, to celebrate an event, or to simply enjoy the beauty of the melody.

The greatest feeling of being a Christian is the promise Jesus made to us all: If we come to Him and believe in Him, He will give us everlasting life. Jesus made that promise and God gave us the Ten Commandments to reinforce the way of salvation. I thank both God and Jesus as often as I can for the opportunity to enjoy eternal life with them, and with my loved ones who have gone before me, and those who will follow.

When God calls out, "Bob, it's time," I will respond without regret, "Lord, I am ready."

. . . for I know whom I have believed,[32] and am persuaded that he is able to keep that which I have committed unto him against that day.

2 Timothy 1:12b (King James Version)

---

32 This Bible verse is also the chorus to the hymn "I Know Whom I Have Believed."

When God Says No

Carol Sedar

Once I read a story about a small girl in Southern California who stood by the living room window praying for a white Christmas. Day after day she faithfully prayed, but snow never came. Her mother said she was sorry that God had not answered her prayer, but the little girl felt differently. She said, "God answered my prayer; He just said, 'No.'"

How do we as Christians make sense of the verse from Psalm 37:4, which states:

Delight yourself also in the LORD,
And He shall give you the desires of your heart.[33]

What if we pray faithfully time after time, sometimes for years, and our prayer goes unanswered, or at least not answered as we wish? We pray for the healing of a daughter with cancer, but the daughter dies. We pray for the healing of a friend with Alzheimer's, but she continues to lose more and more memories. We pray for a family member to accept God into their life, but we see no change. How does this affect our faith in a loving God?

Several years ago our church had a worship service devoted entirely to prayer. Like some others, I went forward to ask that hands be laid on me for healing. My specific prayer was that I could postpone knee replacement surgery for five years, because I was only 55 and the orthopedic surgeon thought I was a little young. At that time they felt a new joint was good for only 15 to 25 years, so it might need to be replaced again in my lifetime. I thought God would hear my plea and the prayers of those faithful

---

33 New King James Version.

friends who had placed their hands on my body and prayed sincerely. But I ended up having the surgery a short while later. I felt that God had not answered my prayer, or at least had said no.

The story, however, does not end there. Probably five years later I was driving home from town thinking about my surgery and my unanswered prayer, and I sensed God whisper, "Carol, I didn't want you to suffer with the pain for five more years." Instead of feeling disappointment, I felt loved by our Lord. It was as though a "no" had turned into a "yes"!

Here is one more story I read years ago. A little girl was looking in a store window and saw a beautiful baby doll in a long white dress. Oh, how she wanted that doll for Christmas! But alas, she did not find it under the tree. Many years later she was attending the baptism of her granddaughter, who was wearing a similar long white dress. She remembered the doll in the window and realized God had given her a much more precious gift.

Lastly, I think of Christ praying in the garden:

He went a little farther and fell on His face, and prayed, saying, "O My Father, if it is possible, let this cup pass from Me; nevertheless, not as I will, but as You will."

Matthew 26:39 (New King James Version)

What if God had removed the "cup," that is, the suffering of Christ on the cross, and thus His resurrection? We would not have the possibility of a personal relationship with God and the chance to join Him in heaven. This "no" became a miracle!

When your prayers are not answered as you wish—when disappointment, trials, or sadness surround you—I pray that you will not give up on God. Sometimes His answers are hard to understand, but He will never abandon you. Trust in His limitless love and care.

Be still, and know that I am God;

Psalm 46:10a (NKJV)

Faith Must Be Based on Evidence

Steven Stiles

I suppose the fact that I was born a pastor's son, spent my entire life in the church, and have no memory of not being a serious Christian qualifies me as a statistical outlier.

This unique life experience had a profound effect on my intellectual development. Early on I grew fascinated not only with world religions, but also with secular-based worldviews, especially those adversarial to Judeo-Christian thought.

Far from disparaging non-Christian perspectives, I have long found myself with a deep appreciation for the complex constructs necessary to interpret a world where the God of the Bible does not exist. Which of these competing perspectives offer humanity the most good and the most meaning in the long view? Why and why not?

What I know and experience as my eternal hope, and indeed the substance of my Christian faith, is in part defined by a growing understanding of what my faith is *not*. So again, I am grateful for those who do not see the world as I do.

Steven Stiles has written several books which are available on Amazon. For example:

Journey on the Hard Side of Miracles, CreateSpace Independent Publishing Platform, third edition (August 15, 2014).

Thorns in the Heart: A Christian's Guide to Dealing with Addiction, CreateSpace Independent Publishing Platform, third edition (August 27, 2014).

Living Today

Anonymous

One big "Ah ha!" in my life came when Sherry McDermott said, "God put your name, all of our names, on a rock."[34] Long ago, before time, my destiny was written. Set. No worries. I am held under God's wing—given shelter, given grace, given enough.

But still, I forget to pray, unless I am in trouble. And then, how bad could trouble be, if it brings me into a conversation with God? I have so much to learn. For example, sex, it turns out, leads to children. . . . You, or at least I, cannot live in a cave and pray all of the time and still keep the children cared for. (Fill in whatever worry of the moment—food, health, bills, more children to care for.)

And I forget another big lesson. God sometimes says, "Maybe later." Not no, not yes, just not now.

Another big lesson is to pause. Consider what the next best thing to do might be. Drink coffee and do that. If it turns out to be a mistake, eat chocolate, walk on the beach.

Another tool is to set up rituals: check blood pressure, check blood sugar, take vitamins, read the Book, start off each day thanking God. Outside. First thing. Maybe start coffee water and then go out and ask God for guidance for the day. Good direction. Listen to my self-will chime in, go with the quiet voice, the surprising intuition. Remember, in my journaling the night before, what my intentions were, and once again turn those over to God. Go with the peace and quiet. My way, my path, was already set. Right? No need to push. The path is prayer.

---

34 See Revelation 2:17.

So the path gets narrower: The children leave home, the house falls apart, the hustle slows down. Walking with the Spirit, I can feel the breeze, see sunshine in dew on the trees, see the miracle of nature as it differs moment to moment. Solidly still in each moment. Here now for me, even though the car needs fixing, I need to haul water, I worry. The solution is to look with awe at the joy in God's world. No worries. Love is all there is. God is love.

I am God's ear to another person who needs connection. We are all one. Like the positive and negative energy in the night sky. We have Life. That is the miracle. Listening to another person's sorrow I can say, "Oh my goodness!" or "That's hard." I can honor the other person by knowing there is a plan.

Here. Now. I honor the humanness of that other person, and in that moment change springs up. The trouble transitions to a lesson about different choices next time. Or it transitions to shared caring. "Sorry your people seem to be going down the wrong path. They'll learn from their mistakes. There is a plan." Or it transitions to memories of grief and loss. "You loved him. You won't lose that. The memory remains." We do this together, and alone start each day thanking God, asking for guidance, being blessed. In a world of 10,000 million dawns, galaxies, and sunrises. In that moment we pause in the flow of God's infinite being.

God walks with us all the time. We are never alone.

Go with God.

Ma Foi, une fois!

Beatrice Easter

Once upon a time, faith was bestowed on a small 4-pound preemie.

Baptized Catholic at two weeks old, a shy girl, I liked going to church. I puzzled at the saints' statues, the smell of incense, the stained glass windows, the nativity scene, Christmas, the beauty and mystery of it all.

Dad, a great pianist-organ master, used to play up on the church's organ and took me to the upper loft, making me feel special. I did not like the image of the crucified Christ, but I loved the story of little Jesus in Bethlehem, the angels, the saints. I did not care for the Latin Mass, but since most of the time I was up with Dad listening to the pipe organ bellow, I enjoyed the service. Everyone around me seemed to have been Catholic for generations.

I got sick a lot with high fevers. One afternoon when alone in bed I felt an angel! I knew about guardian angels and wanted to believe in them, whether they were real or not. My little heart felt I would be okay and not feel so bad. I had tuberculosis when I was two years old, and all kinds of pulmonary and digestive problems. Obviously, I survived!

My first Communion around six years old disappointed me (I thought I would become a saint or something, and the concept of eating the body of Christ was very weird to my young brain). There was no sudden enlightenment as I was expecting. A few weeks later, I lost a cousin when he electrocuted himself in a bath. He was about my age, and I adored him. His death was a big shock and heartbreak, adding to the pain I had already experienced from being sent to a sanatorium at age three (because of the tuberculosis) and the death of my white cat. Two months later, it was my only Grandpa's turn to leave us. Perhaps because of these trials, I became an insomniac at an early age. My Mom used to constantly say that I thought too much.

Unfortunately, from the age of six onward, I was sexually abused by our gardener and an older cousin, and then, as a young teen, by an older brother. All of this covered me with shame and gave me a low self esteem. The Catholic guilt that told me I was a sinner made me feel even dirtier, so I was extremely shy and not well in my skin. By the time of my Confirmation at age 11, I had been taught some good values, such as the commandment to love one another (which puzzled me because I had not learned that God is loving), to be polite, not to lie, to be of service, and so forth; but I was very wounded inside, taking refuge in books and nature.

A week before Christmas, my only Grandma was buried. Then three days later, my oldest brother was in a car accident at age 22. I was left alone at home and got the call that he had died. My idea of God died as well. Having prayed my young heart out when everyone had left to go to the hospital, my grief turned into anger against God and Jesus. I became an avid atheist and devoured all the philosophy books I could put my hands on, never the Bible. I barely knew anything about the Bible except for the New Testament stories, of which the Parable of the Prodigal Son and several others made me cry. Anyhow, between the ages of 11 and 15, I lost three of my oldest cousins, a favorite uncle, and my oldest brother. My parents were so wounded that they went into depression. Books, art, classical music, history, foreign languages inspired me, but I slowly became an existentialist. I loved Sartre and Camus and their atheistic philosophies.

Somehow at around age 13, I started loving to learn English and I bloomed. No longer shy, I became a bit of a social butterfly. I loved news about America and the modern world—lots of beautiful cars, fast planes, no fenced yards, white-toothed smiles, the land of popcorn, ice cream, and abundant wild landscapes. I was also enchanted by stories of Native Americans. One of my favorite cousins came back from a year as an exchange student in the USA. I was hooked! I wanted to do that in a few years. Somehow I figured it out. I studied well—at least in the humanities—and went to England to improve my English skills.

My Dad was extremely proud to send his 17-year-old baby into the big American world. After many interviews I was chosen—one of only three from northern France, out of 300 for the whole country. How exciting! It was the best year of my life, I can still declare. I was open to everything—digesting the culture shock, even the homesickness of growing up, the headaches of figuring out the New York accent after learning proper British English. I was fancy free, no worries. I had a blast! However, three days after I came back from the United States, my Dad died, and again I was angry with God for a few years. I had stopped going to church around age 13.

About a year later I went back to the United States because I loved adventure, and I had to visit California because of all the Eastern mysticism I had heard about. So I hitchhiked from New York to Los Angeles. In New York, a good friend introduced me to the teachings of Guru Meher Baba ("Don't worry, be happy!"). Meditation and the appeal of Eastern culture inflamed me. I had also met "Jesus freaks" in New York, and they intrigued me, but I still hung to the notion that life was not fair, and I carried a negative attitude from seeing both of my parents depressed when I was in my teens. When I was 24, my Mom died after slowly withering away from cancer. I felt really alone and confused. I had no faith in a positive future.

In California, I fell in love with a UC Santa Cruz philosophy student who was a Buddhist. I learned to sit and meditate. Somehow, it did not fit me, and again I drifted. At 25, I was lost, with no faith or hope. Life appeared grim, and I had no direction. A few years later, I ended up back in Santa Cruz, after losing my inheritance because I trusted the wrong people. Later, I became a mother.

My first daughter was simply a miracle, conceived on my first try. I knew I was pregnant right away; I watched a rose slowly open up, and I felt it was symbolic of the fantastic bloom growing inside me. Somehow that triggered a longing to have my baby baptized, because I like tradition, and it was implicit in my family. I started going to Holy Cross Church, as I wished to give my daughter(s) a Christian upbringing with humanitarian visions. I did respect Jesus' commandment to love one another and wanted to share it with my children, even though it is hard to accomplish. Before my brother's death, I had loved Jesus with a child's pure heart, but then it was crushed. Before being a mom, I got involved with a wonderful man who started the St. Francis Catholic Kitchen in Santa Cruz, and through this honorable volunteer work, I was inspired to start praying again. Now 35 years later, I love to meet the homeless/mentally ill on a weekly basis. A simple smile and humane interactions can do wonders.

My life has been a twisted path, with many slaps in the face, detours that were hard to take, losing so many loved ones early on, buckets of tears, loneliness in a foreign adopted country, and so on. But I don't regret any of my hardships, since they made me hopeful in Jesus' promises. Desperate a few times,

I had to fight the bipolar dance and was close to suicide. I humbled myself on the ground before God—and after crying my heart out, I felt some peace. Strange as it sounds, several times, all I had to turn to for comfort was the ground as my solace. I understand the term humble thyself. Somehow after each episode, I was able to pick myself up and continue through my ordeals (dealing with bipolar syndromes in the family, losing property dreams and a great husband too early, to name just a few). My trust in Jesus from childhood came back as I later turned to Bible study. I knew I loved Christ's teachings, but was curious about the ancient book of prophecies and revelations. The Bible was, in my youth, a mystery book, not very clear and slightly taboo.

When my husband got chronically ill and I realized I had no control over my circumstances, I started to pray more in my awkward way. I learned a lot and basically started to trust that I was a child of God. Several times in crisis, I repeated the mantra "Jesus, Mary, Joseph, help me." Once while driving I said this prayer for three hours straight without knowing if one of my daughters would be alive when I arrived. It is not fun to go through so many emotional hardships, yet they allowed me to trust Jesus more as a friend, counselor, and guide.

My volunteer work for the homeless in my community and other involvements with the poor and mentally ill made me realize how spoiled and loved I really am. I learned to accept the lesser ones in our society, not be bothered by their smells or lack of self esteem. Compassion is a wonderful gift that I finally learned over the years. My sense of gratitude started to grow. Several major losses tore me apart, yet I always rebounded and somehow survived. When I began going to Bonny Doon Church, a Protestant church (my parents probably turning in their graves), I finally understood that God *loves me as a daughter*. This was a precious reassurance for someone without parents throughout her entire adulthood. I began to realize that I could have a closer walk with Him who died nearly 2,000 years ago. I could learn to have a personal relationship as I let Him into my heart and allowed His teachings to guide me. This did not always make my life easier. Life's problems did not and will not go away, yet I have the assurance that I am loved with all my flaws, and I am called to be one of His flock. I loved the rituals of the Catholic Church, but it's only within this superb, hilltop, cozy little church and its community that the loving simplicity of Jesus' message started to dwell in my storm-weathered heart.

I regret none of my hardships. I try to put things in perspective. I could have been a refugee, suffered a chronic disease, been born in some slum, been beaten—whatever, there's always something worse. At any rate, at my ripe old age, I learned that God, Jesus, loves me, and my trials are refining me and teaching me not to regret anything and not to be bitter. I know I have no control over the current of my life, and I can trust without worrying about it, each day doing my best to praise and be more grateful. I know that my prayers will not always be answered the way I want, yet giving up control, letting go of fear, and trusting in God have helped me navigate through the crazy waves I have faced. The more I trust and the less I grumble, the less I worry. I have a yearning to be a simple disciple, the lonely sheep looking for safety. Someday I might get to dance with my King and all the angels in Heaven! When I look at the cosmos, I figure there's got to be a happy planet somewhere, and even if it is a fantasy, the idea of Heaven is enticing. The idea of having a soul resonates with me. It truly beats other after-death concepts, such as the nothingness or void of atheism.

Faith is not anything you can see, it is a gift when your heart is ready. I can feel it in my heart. Faith is what keeps me going when others would have given up. It keeps me believing in the goodness of others and helps me find it. Faith is trusting in a power greater than myself and knowing that whatever happens this power will carry me through. Plus, as an avid sailor I know the calm comes after the storm. Faith is peace in the midst of a storm, determination in the midst of adversity, and safety in the midst of trouble. For nothing can touch a soul that is protected by faith. Indeed my faith is a graced gift. Many times I have felt in my heart the rightness of believing Jesus' wisdom, and the scriptures are inspirational. On the next page are a few Bible verses that have blessed my life.

Voilà, my survival story. I am proud to choose not to worry or fear much, because I trust in Jesus' promises! My way of singing praises to God is to stay positive and to keep on smiling.

Though the fig tree may not blossom,
 Nor fruit be on the vines;
Though the labor of the olive may fail,
And the fields yield no food;
Though the flock may be cut off from the fold,
And there be no herd in the stalls—
Yet I will rejoice in the LORD,
I will joy in the God of my salvation.

The LORD God is my strength;
He will make my feet like deer's feet,
And He will make me walk on my high hills.

Habakkuk 3:17–19 (New King James Version)

Do not fear therefore; you are of more
value than many sparrows.

Matthew 10:31 (NKJV)

For I am persuaded that neither death
nor life, nor angels nor principalities
nor powers, nor things present nor things
to come, nor height nor depth, nor any
other created thing, shall be able to
separate us from the love of God which
 is in Christ Jesus our Lord.

Romans 8:38–39 (NKJV)

Trust in the LORD with all your heart,
And lean not on your own understanding;
In all your ways acknowledge Him,
And He shall direct your paths.

Proverbs 3:5-6 (NKJV)

The Knob

Nancy Norris

Here is something God did for me that made me laugh.

Our washing machine died beyond repair, so we cleaned off the stuff we had stored on top of it to make room for a new one. I took my faithful old, highly esteemed friend, my food dryer, and put it on the back seat of our van for the duration. When the new washing machine came, we heaved it into the house, and I built a nice shelf above it for all the stuff we had removed (so it wouldn't vibrate off the machine and onto the floor during the spin cycle). Then I went out to the van to get my food dryer. Alas! One of its two control knobs had vanished. I found that the food dryer would limp along with one knob (you take it off and switch it from place to place), but it felt somehow dishonoring to this nifty old device to be used like that. I asked God, "Lord, would you please send my knob back? I don't, strictly speaking, *need* it, but I really *want* it!" I searched high and low. Then I waited.

A short time later, I drove the van into town. The van was not driving well, so when I got home I popped the hood to see if maybe the woodrat-in-residence had chewed a wire. There were (apparently) no chewed wires, but there *was* my knob, right in the center of the woodrat's nest on top of the engine block! Thank you, God!

The Lord is My Shepherd

Marion Wahl

My Mother was a German-born American who went to Germany to finish her last year of college. That is where she met my Dad. He was a German businessman who had been living in Africa, but had come back to Germany to find a wife. He was looking for someone who would not get too homesick when he took her back to Africa. Henceforth, you guessed it—a perfect pair! My brother Dieter and I were born in southeast Africa, in what I think is now Tanzania.

When World War II broke out in 1939, my father went back to Germany to enlist in the army. My father loved his country, fought for his country, and fairly soon, died for his country on a bitter cold winter battlefield on the Russian Front. (Note: Father was a patriot, not a Nazi.)

My brother Axel was born in Poland, and Dad did get a chance to see him. When Mother's pediatrician warned her that the Russians were breaking through the front, she courageously fled with all three of us. She escaped to our grandmother's home in Rahlstedt, near Hamburg, where we stayed for the duration of the war.

At some point, Mother had lost all her important citizenship papers, so she wrote to the American embassy to be reinstated and allowed to go back to America. The American embassy said, "Yes," and we were allowed to travel to America. This was a HUGE MIRACLE that changed all of our lives! Thank you, Lord! Many people lived in camps for displaced persons for *years* waiting for the opportunity to go to America.

We came over on the old troop ship the *Ernie Pyle* during one of the worst storms on the North Atlantic in 30 years! ☺ Praise the Lord. We were seasick for weeks!

Mother spoke English, but we didn't. She quickly taught us three important words—hello, goodbye, and thank you (pronounced "sank you" in German). We learned English quickly, as it was full-immersion learning. No one dared to speak German after that terrible war, so we were forced to function in English very fast. It did, however, take me two years of speech lessons during elementary school to get rid of my accent. I sounded like Henry Kissinger. ☺

Mother found a job working as a cook for a doctor's family. Since she had to work, Dieter and I were sent to a children's home next to an orphanage. Mother kept Axel with her because he was too young to go to the home. Because I had lost my Dad, and Mother was not around much, I feared that I would die. I was so anxious that I took to my bed. At this point, a loving elderly house mother, Miss Boochie, came and sat at my bedside. She held my hand gently and assured me that Jesus had a better plan for my life, and that He would keep me safe. That was the seed planted in my soul, which sprouted and grew when I began to search for God.

Several years later my aunt and uncle came from California to visit us. And here is another miracle! My uncle by marriage was so enthralled with my brother Dieter that he wanted all of us to come live on his cattle ranch in California. Praise the Lord! You can't imagine how thrilled we were with this new adventure in our lives. Uncle Jim truly made a cowboy out of Dieter as they worked together. I went to high school in Bakersfield, where I was fortunate enough to become part of a water ballet group called the Aquanettes.

I was 10 when we moved from Germany to America and 13 when we came to California. When I was 15, we attended a church that had a vibrant youth group. One day the youth group went on a trip to Huntington Lake. As it happened, the day the group left for the lake, I came down with a terrible sore throat (probably strep). I wouldn't have been able to go *if* it had not been for my mother's perseverance. Sensing my disappointment, she took me to the doctor, who gave me penicillin. Then she called the church office to see if there was anyone who could take me to Huntington Lake. Now, here is another miracle of God's plan. The youth director had been detained and was just about to leave. I got there on a "wing and a prayer"! On the drive up to the lake, the youth pastor turned to me and asked, "Marion, are you saved?" My first thought was, 'Saved from what?'

At Huntington Lake there were lots of teenage kids, perhaps as many as 300 from different churches around the state. We were housed in large tents secured onto wooden platforms, and there were ten cots in each tent. There were many activities at the lake, including water races, which were very invigorating in the ice-cold water. I really didn't know anyone, but everyone was so friendly. In the evening we would gather around a bonfire, sing beautiful hymns, and learn about Jesus and His AMAZING LOVE for us! At the end of that time there was an opportunity for people to commit their lives to Him by taking a little piece of wood and adding it to the fire. On the last day of our time there, I made that commitment and was willing to do whatever and go wherever my SAVIOR wanted. My silent fear of dying was replaced with a new joy of living. Thank you, Jesus, for saving me!

I turned 82 in August of 2019. Praise the Lord! As I look back over my life, I am even more aware of God's AMAZING GRACE! (That is, His undeserved favor to me.)

Here are some of the ways God has blessed me:

- Meeting my sweetheart for life—married 60 years this August (2019). Praise the Lord!
- Having two beautiful, smart, loving, healthy children, a boy and a girl.
- Five wonderful grandchildren who have *all* accepted Jesus as their Savior. (I had the privilege of being there for one!) ☺
- Three adorable great grandchildren.
- On September 28, 1988, the Lord gave me this promise from His word. Isaiah 59:21. It is inside the heart on the facing page. My grandchildren and great grandchildren are all covered under God's grace and this promise to me.
- The privilege of teaching young children at the Bonny Doon School for 25 years!

As you can tell, I count these ALL as miracles and special times in my life.

Our wonderful Lord had
Orchestrated it All!
Even before I knew Him!

"As for Me, this is
My covenant with them," says the LORD:
"My Spirit which is upon you, and
My words which I have put in
your mouth shall not depart
from your mouth, nor from
the mouth of your offspring,
nor from the mouth of your
offspring's offspring," says
the LORD, "from now and forever."
Isaiah 59:21 (NASB)

PRAISE THE
LORD!

According to Merriam-Webster's Collegiate Dictionary, a miracle is "an extraordinary event manifesting divine intervention in human affairs," so you be the judge about these next few miracles in my life.

This one is rather graphic so you will have to steel yourself to continue. . . . ready? 😊 Praise the Lord!

The week before my grandson Jonny's graduation from Westmont College, I had a scheduled colonoscopy with a skilled doctor. The result, he feared, was not good. He had to remove a large growth that he strongly suspected was cancer. And because of its location I might end up needing a colostomy—according to Webster, "a surgical formation of an artificial anus by connecting the colon to an opening in the abdominal wall." In other words, "*the Bag.*" Yikes!

Dick and I, along with our son Steve, were stunned by the news. We prayed about it outside the doctor's office and agreed that we would go to Jonny's graduation and not say anything about my possible cancer until later. We were to see the oncologist the following Monday.

The peace our Lord gave to the three of us was palpable. In John 14:27, Jesus said, "Peace I leave with you, My peace I give to you; not as the world gives do I give to you. Let not your heart be troubled, neither let it be afraid." (New King James Version)

None of us spoke about my colonoscopy again until we were in front of the oncologist's office on Monday. The three of us prayed in the parking lot before going in.

The receptionist was facing us as we arrived. She asked who we were and if we had an appointment. We told her that my doctor had made the appointment for me. She looked for my appointment, came up blank, and mentioned that the doctor had a full schedule and I was *not* on it! Then she had us sit down while she checked with the "very busy doctor." Soon, the receptionist came out and said that the doctor would like to see me, so she ushered us into a small room. By this time we were not only curious, but getting excited about what the Lord had in mind for us. Then this lovely woman doctor came through the door—seemingly more excited than we were—and she said, "The news I'm about to give you, I wish I could give to everyone who comes through my door: YOU DO NOT HAVE CANCER!" Now we were all praising our Lord together!

I could go on to give you many more instances, such as: There was a time when my brother Dieter was in the hospital and his heart stopped twice while he was talking to the doctor. Later, when I went to see him and pray with him, he looked to be in a comatose state with eyes open. I prayed *with* him, *for* him, and *over* him, pleading with God to save his life, *if* that was His will. Months later, Dieter was out of the hospital, had lost 50 pounds, and had lost his diabetes. He was ready to learn to walk again. Praise the Lord!

—And—

How about God's comic relief when I thought I was going to lose my mind staying with my dear Mother, who was by this time suffering from "aggravated depression." I had escaped outside to water her beloved camellias. The water made a tall spray, and I saw a rainbow in the mist. Then the Lord sent this adorable, exquisite hummingbird to fly before my face, so close that I could have kissed him. He flew to the camellia bush, put his chest on a leaf, and slid down like a child would go down a slide. I was awestruck. And just to prove that it wasn't a figment of my imagination, he came over and proceeded to make the same maneuver all over again. By this time, Mother was calling me, and my time there was up.

Last but not least, my younger brother Axel was, I believe, an agnostic, meaning one who is not committed to believing in either the existence or non-existence of God. Basically, I gather he felt that people who believed were weak and needed God for a crutch. I love my brother very much, and I prayed for many years for him to come to know the Lord Jesus personally. By God's amazing grace, when he was 70 years old, he had a Holy Spirit conversion in which he sensed the Spirit of God washing over him. Hallelujah! That was truly a miracle.

Great is God's Faithfulness

Our little Bonny Doon mountain church and the early pastor there, Elwood Hunter, and his wife, Eleanor, played a big part in our lives and in the lives of our children. This continued with God's faithful servants, Pastor John Burke and his wonderful wife, Barbara. The "celestial" church choir was a joy for me to be part of, although I provided their only *flat notes*! They were gracious to me and loved me anyway. Praise the Lord!

But as for me, the nearness of God is my good;
I have made the Lord GOD my refuge,
That I may tell of all Your works.

Psalm 73:28 (New American Standard Bible)

You will make known to me the path of life;

In Your presence is fullness of joy;

In Your right hand there are pleasures forever.

Psalm 16:11 (NASB)

God Cares about Joy

Barbara Gaskell

Many years ago, my husband Martin and I spent a year living on Long Island. At that time we were still a young couple just starting life together and, like many young couples, we didn't have a lot of money for buying non-essentials.

One of the things we loved to do together and with friends was to play music. We had recorders and violins, and we loved singing, but we didn't have a piano or a harpsichord. Deep down inside, we wished we had a harpsichord. Martin grew up playing the piano, so he would be able to play it, and a harpsichord would add so much joy to our music making. There would be so many new musical pieces we could play with friends if we owned a harpsichord.

So we used to joke with one another.

"Where are you going?"

"Oh, I am just going to some garage sales to find us a harpsichord!"

We joked about it, but we didn't actually expect to find a harpsichord at a garage sale, and we didn't feel comfortable praying that God would provide us with one. After all, this was not a necessity; it was just something we really wanted.

But God cares about more than just meeting our basic necessities. He cares about joy. Not our selfish ungodly desires that don't give anything to others, but JOY. He heard this unspoken "prayer"—the prayer of our hearts, not the prayer of our lips—and out of the blue, He gave us a harpsichord! One evening, as we were waiting to go onstage for an early music concert, one of the other participants said, "Would anyone like a harpsichord?" What? Yes! We did!

It turned out this harpsichord was half-built. It was from a "build your own harpsichord" kit that someone had bought in the 1960's and partly finished. At some point the original purchaser decided he needed space in his house more than a half-built harpsichord, so he gave it to his children's school. There it stayed, until the school decided *they* also needed space more than a half-built harpsichord, so they gave it to another of their students' parents. That was how our fellow musician had acquired it. But he was a busy commercial artist and never found time to finish it. Eventually, he too decided he needed space more than he needed a half-built harpsichord.

After ordering some replacement strings and parts, we had that harpsichord working within 24 hours!

We were so excited to receive a harpsichord. We felt that God had given it to us, and it made me feel so loved by God. He *saw* me and He *cared* about me. It wasn't exactly what many would regard as a miracle—certainly no laws of physics were broken—but it *was* unlikely. I mean, hey, how many times in *your* life has someone asked if *you* wanted a harpsichord?

We felt that since God had given it to us, we should do our best to share it with others and use it for God's glory. We have hauled that thing all over everywhere. (It can be moved by two people and a truck.) It has now been in more concerts than we can remember and brought joy to countless musical gatherings both inside and outside of our home. So the next time you hear that harpsichord in Bonny Doon Church, you will know that it was God's special gift to us. Thank you, Jesus!

God Has a Sense of Humor

Barbara Gaskell

One year, when my husband and I and our children were living in Nebraska, money was particularly tight. As a consequence, I began praying the Lord's Prayer, especially the line "Give us this day our daily bread," with some earnestness. I figured if Jesus had told us to pray this prayer, He must be prepared to answer it. A few weeks after I started praying, someone linked me up with a nonprofit called the Food Net, which collected and distributed food that was just past its sell-by date and would otherwise be thrown away by stores.

The very first time I showed up at a Food Net distribution location there was *nothing but bread*—lots of bread, all kinds of bread, some really interesting bread, but *nothing* else. I burst out laughing. I could feel God smiling at me. He loved me. I had complete peace knowing that He was going to take care of me, but I also sensed a delightful twinkle in His eye. It was as if He was saying, "So, are you going to ask Me for anything other than bread?" I laughed all the way home.

After that I asked for my daily vegetables and fruit, as well as bread, and our family began volunteering with the Food Net. During the four or more years that we volunteered, there was never another time when the distribution location had nothing but bread. That first time was the only one. Helping with the Food Net became a source of joy for all of us and a wonderful opportunity for me to teach our children about volunteering and helping others less fortunate than ourselves.

Our chickens liked it too, since they got the leftovers that were too far gone to be eaten by humans.

"And when you are praying, do not use meaningless repetition as the Gentiles do, for they suppose that they will be heard for their many words. So do not be like them; for your Father knows what you need before you ask Him.

"Pray, then, in this way:

'Our Father who is in heaven,
Hallowed be Your name.
Your kingdom come.
Your will be done,
On earth as it is in heaven.
Give us this day our daily bread.
And forgive us our debts, as we also have forgiven our debtors.
And do not lead us into temptation, but deliver us from evil.'

Matthew 6:7-13 (NASB)

Open Prison Doors,
Set the Captives Free

Nancy Norris

My walk with God is in a state of tumult right now, not necessarily bad tumult, but I had hoped things would be a little more settled down before I gave my testimony.[35] I have a fear or longing or suspicion that there is going to be some big sea-change soon. Part of this may involve God getting me out of a certain box I have been stuck in most of my life.

A couple of months ago I had a sort of vision, of a big green joy wave rolling toward Santa Cruz, with light glinting off its sides and a myriad of water voices—splashes and gurgles and roaring. (I saw a similar wave rolling toward the Chowchilla prison.) I thought it meant that God was sending revival here. I don't know what revival is like, but I *think* I long for it and I think it is likely to be tumultuous!

So, about the box.

Suppose you are a two-dimensional creature, say, an ant. You're a two-dimensional ant living in flatland, with lots of other two-dimensional ants. Right now you are imprisoned in a box, which looks like this:

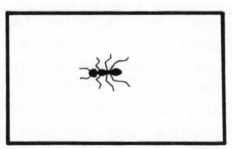

---

35 This story is based on a talk given during a Sunday service at the Bonny Doon Church in 2019.

And you crawl around the edges of the box, feeling for doors or windows. . . . But there aren't any, apparently. You think about calling for help. Maybe someone can come, break down a wall, and get you out? But, oh dear, you can hear bad-guy ants outside talking to each other:

"Dude!"

"Yeah, dude?"

"We got dis place booby-trapped. If anyone tries to break in, da whole place and da stupid ant-dame go kablooey! Ha ha!"

The bad-guy ants forget that God is more than two-dimensional—He can fish you right out of the top of the box.

In my family, periodically, one or the other of us gets stuck in some kind of heavily fortified spiritual box with no doors and no windows. If the prisoner is not me, I say, "Lord, I don't know how you are going to get so-and-so out this time. There just isn't any way, not this time." Then He gets them out, and I am, you might say, bemused. He did it again!

For right now, I am the two-dimensional ant. The box I have been stuck in most of my life goes by the name "naturalism," or physicalism or philosophical materialism. Very briefly, and I'll expand on this later, naturalism is the worldview which says that nature is all there is, there is no supernatural. One flavor says that the most real things in existence are elementary particles, and maybe the laws of physics. It is a bottom-up philosophy: The most real things are elementary particles. These particles bounce off each other and interact, and from that you get physical phenomena. Reality is built from the bottom up: The particles interacting might give rise to chemicals, and the chemicals interacting might give rise to living things, and living things might develop brains, and maybe minds will come out of brains as emergent phenomena. All of reality is built from the bottom up from the truly real things, which are elementary particles. (Does this sound familiar?) By contrast, Christian theism is almost exactly inverted from naturalism. Christian theism says that the most real thing is a Person, namely God. Everything else (including elementary particles) are derivative.

I have lived in naturalism most of my life, but about 40 years ago something happened that made me stop believing that it is actually true, that the world is really like that. But I mostly just can't quite *see* the world as if God is real and in charge, as much as I try. I am really genuinely stuck living in naturalism-landia. Still, I love God desperately and think about him all the time. The really terrific news for me is that God seems to want me anyway, even though I am a bit of a spiritual mess, mostly walking around upside down and seeing His world and Himself in a distorted way.

So what happened to me 40 years ago? The outline is this: One night I was in the basement of a condominium on the edge of a golf course, in Hawai'i. I was praying, which was odd since I was an atheist, and God came right into my naturalism box and did things to it—right there in the basement. I'll tell you about that in a little bit. He took down one wall of my box, very resourcefully getting around the bad-guy ants and the explosive booby-trap. Ever since, he has been coming and going, profligately, in and out of my box, visiting me and bringing me things. About 10 years after God found me in the basement, I gave my life over to Christ, and that made some really wild changes to the occupant of the box (that is, to me). I still live mostly in that box; when I try to walk out of it, it follows me and settles itself around me. This is incredibly aggravating! The felt experience of living inside of naturalism is pretty unsatisfactory; it feels a bit like being shut up all the time in an indoor shopping mall. I have expended huge amounts of effort over the years trying to get out. Maybe soon?

As a philosophy for living one's life, naturalism has some real strengths. One of the gifts it can bring to its adherents is its ability to cut reality down to a manageable size. If you are the kind of person who gets overwhelmed by the huge weighty solemn wildness of existence, you can find shelter in naturalism, where things have sensible explanations or at least the hope of explanation, such as: "Thunder is just sound waves from electrical discharge. Bad dreams are just your brain burning off stress hormones." Another gift of naturalism is that it seems to put a wall between you and "the spookies," that is, unclean spirits or the demonic. You can explain them away, and maybe (if they exist) they really tend not to harass adherents of naturalism. I don't know. The third gift of naturalism I'll mention is that it can filter out a lot of nonsense and untruth. If you are eagerly seeking to discover how the natural world works, you might be drawn to naturalism because it filters out false, illogical stuff. (This works way better with little local phenomena, like thunderstorms, than with big global things, like the meaning of life, where I think naturalism gets reality exactly upside down.)

But as a philosophy for living, naturalism has some peculiar and very unsatisfactory features. I think a lot of us do live in the naturalism box, and this accounts for the pinched faces and deep wistful sadness of so many of us. My daughter Eleanor wrote something like this: "The radical difference between naturalism and most other worldviews is that according to naturalism, the 'Grand Story' of existence and the universe is completely unrelated to what is central to human existence. In naturalism, beauty, meaning, and morals are human constructs." Naturalism has an oddly unmoored quality. In it, the things people most care about—meaning, love, beauty, goodness, life itself—are thought to be local phenomena. Biological life is local to Earth and maybe (wild hope??) to some other planets. Meaning, love, and beauty are found where there are humans and only there, in certain societies and in certain times in the history of the universe. It is as if there are islands of life and warmth floating in a great black dead vacuity. People will give an apologetic laugh and say, "Well, *I* believe in love and goodness (even though I know that it's irrational)." People will say, "I know that there isn't any ultimate meaning in the universe, but really, the universe is handing me the gift and privilege of forging my own meaning, finding a philosophy which is right for me." If you live in naturalism, you have to "settle for." You don't get real beauty or meaning or love; the best you get is the *feeling* of beauty or meaning or love. The whole purpose of your life is to arrange to have the right feelings—feelings of meaning, self-worth, connection with others. But if you hold any of these things in your hand and look at them through the lens of naturalism, they turn into mist and go away. The world gets more and more see-through and less and less solid, until there is nothing there. "A wholly transparent world is an invisible world. To 'see through' all things is the same as not to see."[36]

So there's my box. But what if reality isn't actually like that? There exist some very good philosophical arguments that it isn't. You don't *have* to believe in naturalism in order to be

---

36 From the last sentence of *The Abolition of Man* by C. S. Lewis © 1943 by Oxford University Press.

rational. Eleanor tells me that naturalism's ascendancy seems to be a historical accident. Barbara Gaskell said that when she gave her heart to Christ, the world was flooded with warmth and color and goodness. What if that warmth and color and goodness are not just psychological phenomena but are intrinsic parts of the real world?

In any case, when Jesus started coming in and out of my naturalism box, the box changed: It became lit up and full of glory, even with a crippled occupant. So here's the story about what happened to me in the basement in Hawai'i:

As far back as I can remember in childhood, I had a cheerful confidence in God's nonexistence. The notion that there was someone at the center of reality, doing things, seemed patently silly to me. But a bit farther back than I can quite remember, I was loved and tenderly cared for by the old gray southern California hills I grew up among. I loved the hills in return with all of myself. My siblings and I (often each alone) spent many hours crawling around in great stands of blazing wild mustard, or making nests in the grass, or sitting in special places under the hedges where bits of sunlight lit up spiderwebs. I am surprised that as an increasingly arrogant and contemptuous atheist, I was known and regarded by these hills and by Whoever it was who was walking there.

Two or three times in my childhood I had what I called "wolf moods," when I was out on a little knoll in the wind and got caught up in the huge wild exultant overwhelming glory of things. And two or three times in childhood I had the same dream, a dream about wild geese coming to my yard at night. The dream would take place on a full-moon night, at maybe 3 or 4 in the morning. My family would be standing out on the lawn in the dew, when a great flock of Canada geese (which, by the way, didn't live in southern California) would come swirling through the sky and land on the lawn with us. Then they would talk to us and tell us stories, and take us on short flights on their backs. Finally they would leave, the sun would come up, and we would find, under the eaves, nests of wild birds: sparrows and finches, mockingbirds and mourning doves, with babies. These dreams were more real than real and are among the biggest luminous parts of my childhood. Much later I found out that the wild goose is the Celtic Christian symbol for the Holy Spirit.

We moved to Hawai'i when I was 12. There I spent many hours alone, exploring the pickleweed flats under the sea cliffs up the coast from our house. At night I would sometimes climb out onto the veranda roof below my bedroom, hold my arms up to the sky full of stars, and beg the sky to pick me up. I longed for the sky to gather me up, but I knew that it could not do so.

I was still a committed atheist by the time I was 21 or 22, but my atheism was starting to develop cracks and fissures. The biggest cracks were made by a story or fantasy I had started telling myself. I don't know where the story came from, and the contents are too close to a nerve for me to share much of it. I had two characters: "Myself," a badly damaged, near-mortally wounded 16-year-old girl out in a desert place, and "Linda," a woman of immense goodness and a fair amount of power, seeking to rescue me. I would get all wrapped up in telling myself the story, acting out all the parts in my mind. The woman seemed quite unutterably lovely to me, and I wished. . . I wished that I could be in her presence, or rather, in the presence of someone like her, only more so, and real. This story person loved me, and I began to learn from that what it might be like to be loved by God.

One summer while I was in college, several of us UC Santa Cruz undergrads were invited by a man named Tap Pryor to work as day laborers on an oyster farm he was founding in Hawai'i. So off we went. We'd spend all day cleaning out enormous concrete algae ponds (there were four of them, and each took up an acre of land) or taking care of the baby oysters in their tanks. After work we'd ride bikes (provided by Tap) through a narrow strip of jungle and across a golf course to some condominiums, where we were being housed. Then I would usually go down into the basement of my apartment to work on calculus, which I was trying to learn. The basement had a big plywood bar, stained dark, with a black vinyl bumper around the top and bar stools one could sit on. One night I went down into the basement, and for some reason felt a desire to pray. I had never done that before—I was an atheist, for cryin' out loud!—but there was no one around watching so I knelt down and steepled my hands as I knew one was supposed to do. Imagine my surprise to find that someone was smiling at me from the other side of my closed eyelids! I couldn't see them very well, but they seemed to have a *very* nice smile, and I wondered who they might be. . . . "So, are you God? Or an angel, or whoever is on call in heaven right now, taking prayers from girls in basements? Or my higher self, or an avatar?" Over the next couple of days, I experimented with praying to different people to see if any of them would match the smiling person. I tried praying to myself and to my higher self, but neither matched; and then to an older woman who was a hero of mine—not a match either. Finally I settled on praying to "The Goddess"—not a perfect match, but as close as I could get back then.

So it was down there in the basement that my world cracked open, and acres of light came pouring in through the crack.

I had not become a Christian. Looking back, I wonder if what happened was that I had fallen in love with Jesus—completely, head over heels. If so, God very wisely did not rub my face in it. Remember the bad-guy ants? Well, the booby-trap in my box was a fear of being shamed. There is a high probability that if someone from my little subculture of America becomes a Christian, they will be subject to contempt and shaming from their fellows. Barbara, who beat me to Christianity by 10 years or so, probably took the worst of it, so when I came along, it was way easier. In my case the contempt would not have come from my family but from my intellectual community. Since my entire sense of worth and dignity was wrapped up in that community, it would have been rough. But God *didn't* tell me, "Hey Nancy! Guess what? You've fallen in love with Jesus!" So He was able to take down the front wall of my box without the box or inhabitant (me) getting blown up.

So I had not become a Christian, but I started praying, about two minutes a day. I'd go to quite a bit of trouble to sneak off by myself for those two minutes. Sometimes I'd tell my housemates that I was going out to say goodnight to the moon. Or if it was raining, I'd go into the bathroom and lean on the door so no one could get in, and then I'd pray.

I started attending Quaker meetings, and eventually, 10 or 15 years after the basement incident, I took a prayer class and joined a prayer group led by the Princeton Quaker Meeting. And I kept telling myself the story which had started it all.

From all of this, I came down with a horrible case of unscratchable God-itch. I wanted God. I wanted God's company. I wanted to be much closer to God than I could seem to get.

So I wrote a letter to my little sister, Barbara, complaining about this. She wrote back saying, "Nancy, if you want to get close to God, you're probably going to have to go through Jesus." Hmmmm. . . . I thought about this for a year or two. (I can hardly believe how patient God has been with me.) Then I began to ask myself, "Nancy, do you remember that person in your story? The one whose company you long for? Isn't that person in a lot of ways rather reminiscent of . . . Jesus? OH NOOOO!!!!" I thrashed around in confusion for a time over my story-person being female and Jesus being male, but finally my intense longing won out over my confusion and embarrassment and fear of self-delusion, and at long last I said "yes" to Jesus.

People report that when they say "yes" to Jesus, He becomes nearer than breathing, and He opens a spring of living water in their soul. Well, they are right. Directly after I invited Jesus in, my unscratchable God-itch went away, never to return. This is not because it was anesthetized, but because I can scratch it now. I still often poignantly long for God's company, but there has been an absolutely tremendous change in my life. I can feel the living water in my middle. I could and can feel the in-rushing and infilling of life.

It says in 2 Corinthians 5:17 that one becomes a new critter in Christ. That is true; one becomes (probably gradually) a really lovely kind of creature, probably the kind of creature God intended one to be in the first place. I picture (and this is just an image) something diaphanous, with a lot of light inside. Eleanor had an interesting experience. She was over at Cabrillo College and saw a young man, too far away to make out his face, but he had light pouring out of him. When Eleanor got closer she saw that it was a Godly young man named Raphael.

In Christ, one gets what seems to me like the coolest job going. I picture (and again, this is just an image) that God has handed me a device sort of like a flashlight, from which God's blessings pour out. Sometimes I wave my device around profligately, aiming God's blessing at just everything. Gradually the place or person so blessed seems to change, starting to shimmer with beauty and holiness. Some of us have walked up and down our road, praying, for years, and I think our road has changed in that same way.

Now about that box. Sometimes lately I have managed to step just outside my box, and I am amazed and frightened by how big the world is—solemn and weighty, with dark canyons and great cliffs with light pouring down their faces. And the world is full of Someone or someones. Then I get scared and run back inside my box.

Eleanor told me with some urgency, "Mommy, you don't want to just run *from* naturalism into the big world out there, because the big world contains real evil, and you could get hurt. The only safe thing to do is to run *to* Jesus."

Barbara told me a story which I don't think she put in her testimony, so I'll end with Barbara's story. She pictured herself and me as being like immigrants to Christianity from the "old country." Since we immigrated to Christianity as adults, we are a bit clumsy in our new country. Things our kids (who grew up here) find easy, we may find hard. We have accents from the old country that never completely disappear. But the really amazing thing is that God wants us. He really wants us, even though we talk funny and are spiritually crippled and maybe accidentally insult Him at times. In glory we'll be beautiful. In the meantime, He wants us, broken feathers and all.

And Can It Be?

by Charles Wesley[37]

Long my imprisoned spirit lay
Fast bound in sin and nature's night.
Thine eye diffused a quick'ning ray:
I woke—the dungeon flamed with light!
My chains fell off, my heart was free,
I rose, went forth, and followed Thee.

Amazing love! how can it be
That Thou, my God, shouldst die for me!

---

37 Verse 3 in *The Hymnal for Worship and Celebration* © 1986 WORD
MUSIC. The words to this hymn are in the public domain.

Naturalism:
It Just Isn't Natural

Eleanor Littlestone

Exploring what modernity's dominant worldview says to my generation's longing for social justice[38]

"He has, after all, a place in the universal order of things. The stars, the black skies affirm his humanity, his validity as a human being. He knows that his belly, his lungs, his tired legs, his appetites, his prayers and his mind are cherished in some profound involvement with nature and God."

John Howard Griffin, from *Black Like Me*[39]

Some things are easier to see than others. And often the most invisible things have the most power because they are invisible.

When I first came to Cabrillo Community College, I was greeted by chalk messages on the sidewalks. They were about suicide—honoring its victims and affirming the worth and validity of those who had taken their lives and those struggling with suicidal depression. Everywhere the campus seemed bathed in solemn struggle: the struggles of those from all walks of life seeking education, and the struggle to make space for the oppressed and marginalized. The posters, the events in the quad, the signs declaring it a safe space—everywhere was visible the longing in my generation's heart for social justice. But half-invisible things are acting on that longing, even denying its validity. Those half-invisible things are some of our society's fundamental presuppositions about the world: in particular, the

---

38 This story was modified from a college paper.
39 From *Black Like Me* © 1960 by John Howard Griffin.

view of naturalism, which in modern times has superseded religious views as the dominant world-picture. I believe that naturalism is deeply inadequate because it cannot account for intrinsic human worth. And intrinsic human worth is central to my generation's longing for social justice.

It is a familiar concept today that we all see the world through culture-specific glasses. Our understanding of things is "tainted" by the background beliefs, assumptions, and ways of thinking of a given society. These assumptions, although familiar within the society which holds them, are elusively difficult to see. As Kant noted, we cannot see them because they are the concepts through which we see everything else.[40]

Every generation, I think, has its special gifts and curses bestowed on it through its unique place in the history of humanity. Each generation is born into a certain stream of politics, debates, ideas, pressures, and cross-pressures. I think my generation's gift is that of perceiving the importance of human identity. Being myself part of my generation, I have learned this through friendships, classmates, and innumerable conversations. But even more, I have learned it from leaders of InterVarsity, an organization that creates spaces for dialogue with students about spirituality, social justice, and what is meaningful in their lives. Philosopher Charles Taylor, an expert in modern secular culture, calls this the "Age of Authenticity":[41] an age of seeking to be fully ourselves and not be crushed by societal structures which threaten to invalidate us, or tell us to deny parts of ourselves that are deep and precious and fundamental. To this generation, it is a terrible thing to invalidate someone's identity, because that

---

40 Matson, Wallace I. *A New History of Philosophy: From Descartes to Searle.* Harcourt College Publishers, 2000, page 456.
41 Taylor, Charles. *A Secular Age.* The Belknap Press of of Harvard University Press, 2017.

person, the way they really are—not the way anyone else says they should be—is a vastly important and serious matter. This has its anchor in a conception that every human being has, as sociologist Christian Smith describes, "an inherent worth of immeasurable value ... [which] makes persons innately precious and inviolable."[42] Every person has immense worth simply because they are human. I will henceforth call this "intrinsic worth."

This conception of intrinsic worth is the foundation of my generation's longing for social justice. We long to uplift minorities, to give a voice to the forgotten and despised and outcast, to lament those oppressive systems which crush them because we know all humans matter and their identities are precious. Looking around my school, we find an advocacy club for people with disabilities, and another seeking to reduce the stigma around mental illness. Even the fierce debates between those who are pro-life and pro-choice stem from each side's belief in intrinsic worth: the one defending unborn babies, the other defending women. There is my own InterVarsity, a Christian organization, reaching out to the LGBT+ community with love and respect, because it, as a faith-based organization, is lamenting the deep wounds other Christians have given them.

But to my generation it is also common knowledge that all values are invented by humans—they are human "constructs." As Timothy Keller explains, "All morals, we believe, should be chosen by us individually or perhaps by our culture collectively."[43] Social constructs, human constructs, subjective

---

42 Smith, Christian. *What is a Person?: Rethinking Humanity, Social Life, and the Moral Good from the Person Up.* The University of Chicago Press, 2010, page 435.
43 Keller, Timothy. *Making Sense of God: Finding God in the Modern World.* Penguin Books, 2018, page 179.

feelings—that is the language of today, and it arises from modernity's half-hidden presuppositions about the world. It comes from modernity's dominant paradigm of naturalism, which I shall define presently. Naturalism's influence, I think, is the "curse" part of my generation's package, for naturalism severely weakens the concept of intrinsic human worth.

Ask yourself if the following ideas are familiar:
- It is up to us to create our own values and meaning.
- Science has superseded religion, and scientific explanations are the only really valid knowledge.
- Values are distinct from fact.
- Beauty, meaning, and morals are human constructs.

These ideas all stem directly from naturalism. Naturalism is a philosophical position. It is a worldview in the sense that it provides an overarching framework for explaining and understanding what the universe is, what life is about, and how we can gain knowledge about what exists. Philosophers J.P. Moreland and William Lane Craig, who have written extensively on the subject, list the following features as characterizing naturalism. First, there is no God or spiritual beings or anything "supernatural"; all that exists is matter and energy. Second, only those things discoverable through our five senses and the scientific method are real. This means, for instance, that there is no such thing as "beauty" lurking out there in the universe, since it is not something which can be touched or smelled or measured or weighed. Interactions between light, molecules, and neurons in the brain produce the subjective *experience* of beauty, but independently of that, beauty does not exist. The same goes for other non-material realities such as love and values. They are not real entities in the furniture of the universe since they are outside the realm of physical reality discoverable through science. According to naturalism, beauty, love, and values are all human constructs.

Finally, in the same way as Christianity posits a "Grand Story" of the universe involving creation, Jesus's birth, and so on, naturalism has a view of the universe's "Grand Story": The universe does not exist for a purpose; it just is, and its history and future are defined by a chain of cause and effect according to the laws of physics. Life on earth emerged as part of this physical process, and the story of humanity's existence is fully that of evolutionary biology. All that is to be known about the story of the universe and humanity is hypothetically knowable through science.[44]

The radical difference, then, between naturalism and most other belief systems or worldviews is this: Naturalism's "Grand Story" is completely unrelated to what is central to the experience of human existence. To understand this, let's look at some other worldviews. In Christianity, the universe exists because it is created by God, out of love, for a purpose. The ultimate reality behind everything is a person acting with intention, even as we on the small local scale are persons acting with intentions toward purposes. Since we were created for a purpose, there is also good and bad: good being the way things are meant to be and bad being the opposite. So value and purpose exist at the human scale because they exist at the grand scale. Similarly, C.S. Lewis writes of Hinduism: "Conduct in men which can be called good consists in conformity to, or almost

44 Craig, William Lane, and J.P. Moreland, editors. *Naturalism: A critical analysis*. Routledge, 2000, page *xi*.

participation in, the Rta—that great ritual or pattern of nature and supernature which is revealed alike in the cosmic order, the moral virtues, and the ceremonial of the temple."[45] The same is true, Lewis writes, of Platonic, Aristotelian, and Stoic philosophy.[46] Even with The Force in *Star Wars*, the value and purpose inherent in our humanity are reflected on the cosmic scale, for from The Force come good and evil. In all these diverse philosophies, purpose and value—so central to our existence—are central also to the existence of all reality.

Now enter naturalism. The universe is a brute fact, and we ourselves arose as part of the long line of physical causes and effects which had no purpose in mind. Thus it turns out the value and purpose so central to our humanity are merely by-products of this process. Where other worldviews point beyond the local human world of values and purposes to those same things in larger and fuller form, naturalism looks beyond and finds they are "really just": It *seems* like I have an immortal soul, but it's "really just" brain chemistry. My love for my friends *seems* real, but it's "really just" due to my evolution as a social animal because socialness helped my ancestors survive. This led Christian Smith to comment: "[Naturalism] cannot recognize, much less adequately understand and account for, immaterial realities, like value, meaning, morality, and personhood. So it is stuck with the . . . task of denying, reducing, eliminating, and explaining away . . . that which is often most important in human life."[47] Where other worldviews look outside of human experience to explain immaterial realities like love and morality, naturalism looks outside of human experience to explain such things away.

---

45 Lewis, C.S. *The Abolition of Man.* Harper Collins, 2001, page 17.
46 Lewis, page 18.
47 Smith, *What is a Person?* page 114.

But that which makes up the essence of human experience will not be done away with so easily. Rather, naturalism relocates it. If it is not sewn into the fabric of the universe, it is in the fabric of our subjective experience. If it is not real the way a water molecule is real, it is nonetheless very real to us. So the embrace of naturalism involves a radical relocation of values, a shift from outer to inner, objective to subjective. What is lost is "the doctrine of objective value, the belief that certain attitudes are really true, and others really false."[48] With this loss, we have the freedom and obligation to create our own meaning and to project that meaning onto a meaningless universe. Those are the two sides of naturalism's coin.[49]

In naturalism, the value of human beings—that intrinsic worth—shares the same fate of all values. The universe did not create humans for a purpose. There is no God in whose image we are made. The blind forces which brought us forth cannot endow us with worth, purpose, or meaning since they have none themselves. They care about nothing and pass no judgment, because they are not a conscious being. It is up to humans to declare ourselves worthy.

To my generation, this idea of ourselves as creators of our own meaning is common sense. Furthermore, it tends to be viewed as a good thing, a triumph over the past. For the concept that values and human purpose are reflected in a "cosmic order" demanding our allegiance has a troubled history. With so much war and hatred over religious differences, the idea of objective values can seem inherently problematic. It creates division: If there is only one way to salvation or truth, some are on the right path and some are not. If there are objective moral standards,

48 Lewis, page 18.
49 Taylor, page 581.

some people will follow them and some won't. There are outsiders and insiders, and the in-groups can hate the out-groups. One young adult articulated my generation's wariness of objective values this way: "You know, some of these people are so firm in their beliefs. I find that that's contributed to a lot of the problems that we see today, and maybe not on such a minuscule scale. So maybe [my view is] just a commitment to not imposing your beliefs, or trying to dominate other people, or trying to control people."

But maybe this move is like some surgeries. If an organ has cancer, you can get rid of it by removing the organ. But without that organ, there are things the body cannot do. I now ask, without objective standards, can we get to the idea of intrinsic human worth?

I posed this question in an interview with Barbara Gaskell, a person familiar in a uniquely personal way with the philosophy of naturalism. Raised in a world of philosophical and intellectual discussions and within a worldview of naturalism, she is now a Christian theist. Today the contrast between naturalism and theism is one of her great interests. Radiating comfortable warmth, she speaks slowly and softly, putting thought into every word. One can get most of the way there (to intrinsic worth) she tells me. If we look inside ourselves we have a strong sense of our own worth, and from this, through the capacity of empathy, we impute worth to other humans. But, she says, "There's a sort of limit. You can get closer and closer to the limit but you're never going to get there, because if you're going at it from that angle you can only get so far." Naturalism, Gaskell says, can get us morals and law codes and respect for our fellow humans. It can get us human flourishing. But what it cannot do is "get you the last, final step that says that other people have intrinsic value apart from what I impute to them or what other people impute to them, just because they exist."

True. According to naturalism, the existence of human worth depends on someone believing in its existence. It is a human construct, valid so long as there are humans available to consider it real. But does this make any difference? Does it make a difference if something is real—part of the fabric of the external universe, the cosmic order? Why does it matter if it is real, so long as it feels real to us?

The problem with things being human constructs is they do not exist at all if there is no one around to construct them. And the implications of this problem—that values don't exist unless humans construct them— run completely counter to what we are longing for. Suppose Hitler had taken over the entire world and managed somehow to make every person alive believe all the atrocities he committed were morally right. Now, according to naturalism, in this hypothetical world what Hitler did would be right. Values are human constructs, and in this world there would be no human being available to construct a system of values which says Hitler was wrong.

OK. That's the logical conclusion of naturalism in some far-fetched, abstract way. But the actual world, for all its ugliness, has never been quite that misled. And if it ever were, how would even objective values save us? In the actual world, when we acknowledge human worth to be a human construct, we are also acknowledging that we care about it. We *do* care about it. Of course we care about it. Why bother with all that abstract Hitler stuff?

But it is not that easy. The Hitler thought experiment is all too close to reality. My generation is full of passion for equality for women. Although there is plenty of opposition, women's rights is a concern which a great many consider important and valid. What, though, if the movement for women's rights had never begun? What if it had never become part of society's consciousness that something was terribly wrong with the old system? What if history had gone on its way, unperturbed? We want to think that would have been tragic, horrible, completely wrong. But naturalism will not let us. We can say we *feel* it would have been tragic, that from our current cultural vantage point and system of values we find such an idea horrible. We can say, "today, from within our culture, we consider it tragic." But that is all.

There are many individuals and cultures with many different constructs of values. How do we say whose ideas are superior? The majority's? The most culturally acceptable? But then the slaveholders in the South and the Nazis would have been in the right in certain locations and points in history. Who is the arbiter? All humans are humans. Where do we get this judgment, as though from over and above humanity? Naturalism did away with such judgments.

In a study of 18- to 23-year-olds' moral views, Christian Smith found that 60 percent were "moral individualists," believing each person's moral beliefs and judgments are neither inferior nor superior to anyone else's. This is right in line with naturalism. "They said that morality is a personal choice, entirely a matter of individual decision," writes Smith. "Moral rights and wrongs are essentially matters of individual opinion, in their view."[50] At the extreme end, Smith encountered one young adult who believed he could not judge the wrongness of slavery for 19th century Americans. "Who am I to judge?" This person explained. ". . . I wasn't alive back then, so I can't really pass

---

50 Smith, Christian, with Kari Christoffersen, et. al. *Lost in Transition: the Dark Side of Emerging Adulthood*. Oxford University Press, 2011, page 21.

judgment on it, though in today's world I think it'd be utterly ridiculous, like I wouldn't agree with it. But, like I said, it's society, it changes."[51] Another interviewee expressed similar thinking about terrorists. "It's not wrong to them. They're doing the ultimate good. They're just like, they're doing the thing that they think is the best thing they could possibly do and so they're doing good . . . do we have any idea if it is actually wrong to murder tons of people?"[52] Smith writes that my generation is morally confused and inconsistent, having opinions about values but no foundation on which to hang them.[53] Yes, my generation has a gift of perceiving the worth of humans, but cannot say such recognition of worth would matter if they were not there to care about it. Writing in chalk that transgender women are loved, crying over the horrors of racism, and then throwing up our hands and admitting these things wouldn't matter if we weren't here to care—those things just don't sit comfortably together. We want to say transgender women matter, and they always mattered, and they would matter no matter what. We want to say racism is ugly. Period. We want a kind of human dignity and worth which exists no matter what society thinks, regardless of anyone's opinion.

Naturalism's take on human worth is crushingly disappointing in the same way it would be if I were in love with someone and it turned out he was imaginary:

How well I know my true love's voice, if I hear it all my heart rejoices. How well I know that golden-brown hair, and the warmth that hangs about him like all the fragrances of summer. But then I am informed that, by some odd quirk in my genetics, I

---

51 Smith, *Lost in Transition*, page 27–28.
52 Smith, *Lost in Transition*, page 28.
53 Smith, *Lost in Transition*, page 60.

hallucinated him. "It was a vivid experience, we know, but he is only a construct of your brain. There is no such man." But they have comfort for me also. "It's really all right," they tell me. "He's very real to you. Just look within yourself. He will always be there, your deep treasure, a reflection of your deepest self and your deepest love. It's really better this way, too. Real men have problems, and you won't always agree with them, or like what they are doing. This way he'll always be just the way you want him to be."

I would find that no comfort at all. In the same way, intrinsic worth that is not *real* is hardly intrinsic worth at all.

Now, according to modernity's typical narrative, this is just our tough luck. We happen to exist as beings who long for worth and meaning and value in a meaningless universe which cares nothing about our existence. The story of modernity is seen as a kind of coming-of-age of the human race: throwing off the comfortable illusions of childhood, becoming old enough to face the truth that what we love is not reflected in a cosmic order, and in the face of this absurdity creating our own meaning.[54] However, I want to suggest instead that naturalism's failure to account for what we know to be true (like intrinsic worth) is a failure of naturalism as a theory. A worldview that explains away the most important parts of human existence might not be the best account of our world. When we are seeking knowledge of the world, we should seek a theory that provides the best account of what we want to explain. We have good reasons to believe intrinsic human worth is real. If this reality is dependent on the reality of objective values, this suggests objective values are *also* real and naturalism is false.

---

54 Taylor, Charles. *A Secular Age*. The Belknap Press of Harvard University Press, 2017, page 588.

Taylor observes that the plausibility of naturalism lies not in its intellectual credentials, but in the way its narratives have woven themselves into our intellectual history. Naturalism's narratives "function as unchallenged axioms rather than as unshakable arguments, and . . . they rely on very shaky assumptions."[55] Nor is naturalism necessarily the most "scientific" position. Countless scientists, past and present, perceive the findings of science as pointing toward a supernatural reality, or in any case, as not denying such a reality. Sociologist Elaine Ecklund writes that almost 50 percent of elite scientists are affiliated with a religion.[56]

Calling objective values human constructs is like writing a fantasy game on the computer. If you create your own virtual reality you can make it however you want. You can have whatever you want. You can be free. But only in imagination. And in the end, you never get what you want at all, because what you get does not exist. For it is only a game, only inside the computer, and only those who *want* to will play it. As much as you play your fantasy game, other people on other computers will still be playing theirs. They are all separate imaginary worlds: each with their own standards. Maybe we began to play the fantasy game because we thought what we longed for was not real. But what if it is just outside the window? What if we got up, drew back the curtains, and looked—and what if we found it, after all?

---

55 Taylor, page 590.
56 Ecklund, Elaine Howard. *Science vs. Religion: What Scientists Really Believe.* Oxford University Press, 2010, page 33.

O LORD, You have searched me and known me.
You know when I sit down and when I rise up;
You understand my thought from afar.
                . . . .
Such knowledge is too wonderful for me;
It is too high, I cannot attain to it.
Where can I go from Your Spirit?
Or where can I flee from your presence?
If I ascend to heaven, You are there;
If I make my bed in Sheol, behold You are there.
                . . . .
For You formed my inward parts;
You wove me in my mother's womb.
I will give thanks to You, for I am fearfully and
        wonderfully made;
Wonderful are Your works,
And my soul knows it very well.
My frame was not hidden from You,
When I was made in secret,
And skillfully wrought in the depths of the earth;
Your eyes have seen my unformed substance;
And in Your book were all written
The days that were ordained for me,
When as yet there was not one of them.

How precious also are Your thoughts to me, O God!
How vast is the sum of them!
If I should count them, they would outnumber the sand.
When I awake, I am still with You.

                Psalm 139 verses 1-2, 6-8, 13-18 (NASB)

God Won

Barbara Gaskell

I grew up in a happy family of agnostics. They were all kind, caring, and honest people, who were not opposed to religion, but who generally felt that people became religious because they wanted something to lean on (especially my father). In other words, they felt that God didn't actually exist, but humans had invented the idea of God because the world is a scary and dangerous place. People wanted help, and they wanted something that would make them feel secure and give them comfort. The unspoken background assumption was that religion was for "weak" people. Strong people, "like us," were able to stand on their own two feet and didn't need religion. Since I didn't want to be seen as weak, this prevailing family attitude kept me from seriously exploring anything religious for many years. It wasn't until I had moved away from home and was living on a college campus, that I finally had the courage to try to discover for myself what I believed about God.

But before I get to that, let me backtrack just a little. When I was 10 years old, our next door neighbor, and my mother's best friend, invited me to come to church with her family. I went faithfully to their church for a whole year. My parents didn't mind. My Mom had also grown up attending an assortment of churches. My neighbor took me to an Episcopal church in a pretty building with stained glass windows and a lovely organ. I never stayed for the whole service because children were sent off to Sunday school after the opening hymns, but I found the first part of the service quite moving. The beautiful building, the organ, and the swelling voices of the congregation lifted my spirits, and made me wonder what or who was out there. I tasted something in that church that I wanted, that some deep down part of me longed for intensely, but I didn't know what it was, and I never found it while I was there. After that first year, our family moved to another state and I never went to church again, but this church continued to influence my life.

The most significant thing that happened while I was attending the Episcopal church came as a surprise. I won a contest! It was a coloring contest, and as a prize I was given a copy of an excerpt from the Prayer of St. Francis printed on a lovely cloth wall hanging.

> Lord make me an instrument of your peace.
> That where there is hatred, I may sow love,
> That where there is wrong, I may sow the
> spirit of forgiveness.
>
> . . . .
>
> For it is by giving that we receive.
> It is by forgiving that we are forgiven,
> And it is by dying that we awaken to eternal life.

I loved that prayer! I hung it immediately on my bedroom wall and read it over and over. For many years, that wall hanging was my only link to God, and it became very precious to me. I can remember reading that prayer several years after I had received it and being moved to tears. I *wanted* God, but I thought that I couldn't have Him because my parents knew that He didn't exist. I was quite sure they were right. After all, they were both smart scientists.

The Episcopal church also gave me a Bible, but unfortunately it didn't do me much good. It was the King James

Version, and the old language was a real barrier to my young mind. This translation is beautiful, especially to those who grew up with it and are familiar with the way it sounds, but to someone coming from a family of agnostics, it was like trying to read a foreign language. I read from the beginning of Genesis all the way to chapter five until I encountered "so-and-so begat so-and-so." I didn't know what the word "begat" meant, and at the age of 10, I was too lazy to get out a dictionary, so I never read any further. Instead I looked at the pretty pictures, filled out the family tree in the center, and deposited the Bible on the bookshelf where it remained unopened for years.

I did still occasionally pray for things but without much success (at least that I could see). When I was 11, we spent six months living in Chile. We lived near the beach, and one day my father brought home a sick shore bird. I passionately wanted that bird to live, so I hid under the dining room table and prayed intensely for God to heal it. But the bird died. I was so disappointed, not only that the bird had died (which made me cry), but also because there didn't seem to be anyone out there hearing my prayer. I concluded that my parents were probably right that God didn't exist, and after that I rarely prayed about anything.

By the time I started college I had fully absorbed my family's agnosticism and was satisfied with it. The idea that humans had invented religions out of a desire to manipulate our mysterious and not always pleasant circumstances seemed logical and well supported. Evolution had, for mysterious reasons of its own, given us large brains, and large brains had enabled us to ask difficult questions about pain, death, and dying. The variety of religions in the world suggested a multiplicity of human attempts to wrestle with these questions, and also suggested that there was no obvious right answer. I no longer felt any longing for God. After all, at that age the world is opening up before you and there are thousands of lovely things to explore. But the question remained in the back of my mind, now more as a matter of simple curiosity. Does God exist? Is He real, or just a human idea?

When I was in my sophomore year of college, I decided that the time had finally come to tackle this question, so I set aside a page of my journal, labeled "God." Every time I thought of an argument or any evidence for or against the existence of God, I wrote it down on this page. I kept this up for almost a year, and some time in the middle of my junior year settled down with my journal to see what I had come up with.

In God's providence, during that same junior year I also happened to be studying introductory physics. It is interesting to me that God used a field of science, the very thing that was my biggest barrier to belief, to give me permission to consider His existence. I know that probably sounds odd, so let me try to explain.

During my first quarter of physics in college, we learned mathematical rules and equations that can be used to describe the movement of objects in the natural world around us—otherwise known as classical mechanics. Classical mechanics is logical and intuitive. We instinctively understand how balls bounce, why arrows must be shot high, and why we lurch forward when the car brakes are applied. So much of what we daily experience as we go through life is accurately described by classical mechanics. Great! I liked that about physics. It made sense. But the next quarter we moved on to relativity, and in relativity I discovered something almost as difficult to understand as God. We had problems to solve like, "If a witch on a 10-foot broomstick flies through an 8-foot-long barn at near the speed of light, will she and her broomstick fit inside the barn?"[57] Huh? How does that make sense? Relativity is *not* intuitive; it is difficult to wrap our brains around, but it is scientifically true. Wow! Did that mean that other difficult, non-intuitive things, like God, could also possibly be true? At the very least, the fact that I couldn't wrap my brain around God did not automatically prove that He was an idea invented by humans.

Pondering all this made me realize that although science could not be used to prove the existence of God, it also couldn't *disprove* the existence of God. The idea that God might exist wasn't really any weirder than some of the scientific ideas I had run across studying relativity. It was with that background that I sat down to look at the page in my journal labeled "God." What had I come up with? The answer was—almost nothing. It all fit quite comfortably on less than one page. I had thought of very few arguments either for or against God. Interesting! I learned one useful thing from this exercise: While I could not think of any solid reasons why I *should* believe in God, I also didn't have any good reasons for *disbelieving* in God. For the first time in my life, I had come to a place of true neutrality. I was in the middle, not knowing which way to go.

Agnosticism, where I had been before, is—from a practical point of view—not much different from atheism. An agnostic is living life and making decisions as if God does not exist. But true neutrality doesn't provide any framework for

---

57 The answer is: Yes, you could see her entirely inside the barn. In fact, you could simultaneously close both doors while she was whooshing through. For more information, see "The Ladder Paradox" in Wikipedia.

decision making. I was left dangling in mid-air without any basis for knowing which way to go.

It is hard to describe to anyone who hasn't been there just how uncomfortable this place is. Almost every decision we make in life depends on our belief framework. With no framework, it was impossible to decide anything. I couldn't go either forward or backward—I couldn't do anything at all.

The discomfort of that situation left me rather desperate to find some way of resolving the question, but I felt at a loss. It seemed so impossible to figure out. Finally, I found something in one of my sister Nancy's writing books that seemed to offer a way out. It was a description of what the author called "the believing game." It went like this:

Suppose you are looking at something that is too far away to see clearly. It looks like a fuzzy blob. How do you go about deciding what it is? Well, scientists claim that with our unconscious minds we make a guess. We say, "Maybe that fuzzy blob over there is a horse?" Then our minds superimpose an image of a horse on top of the fuzzy blob. If the fuzzy blob really is a horse, the superimposed image combines with the real image, and we are suddenly able to see it. If the blob is not a horse, it will remain fuzzy, and our minds make another guess —"Maybe it's a dog," and so forth. My father later confirmed that this is in fact what our minds do, but it happens so fast that we are not consciously aware of it.

I was intrigued by this idea, and I decided to apply it to God. It was the closest thing I could think of to a scientific experiment for determining whether God existed. I said to myself, "I know what the world looks like through the eyes of 'there is no God' because I have lived my whole life with that framework. I have all the pieces arranged and fit into their places, just so. It makes sense to me and seems satisfactory. But I don't know what the world looks like through the eyes of 'there is a God.' In fact, I can't even imagine what it looks like that way. So perhaps I should live my life as if 'there is a God' until I can see *that* worldview from the inside. Then I will take these two worldviews, hold them up side by side, and see which one makes everything clearer—which one makes better sense—just see how they compare." That was the basis on which I crossed the line from agnosticism to theism. It didn't mean that I knew that God existed, only that I had decided to live, in a practical way, as *if* He existed, and see what happened.

So one morning (the Saturday of Memorial Day weekend, 1978), I sat down in front of my bed and told God that if He existed, He could have my life and I was going to do my best to follow him. (Martin[58] remembers that he was praying for me that morning.) I was afraid. I didn't know what would happen when I did this. If God did not exist then nothing would happen, but if He *did* exist then *anything* could happen, and *anything*, when it is a big unknown, is pretty scary. I wondered if God would squash me or dominate me. Would I be able to change my mind if I didn't *like* God?

What helped me overcome my fear was the strong sense that God was Himself in the room with me. He was smiling at me with love in His eyes, and He was waiting patiently to see what I would do. He knew me, inside out and backwards, and He still loved me. He didn't say anything. He was just waiting, and His presence filled me with both joy and longing. I wanted Him, and that desire was stronger than my fear. I still wasn't a hundred percent certain that I wasn't just imagining Him, but His presence felt so very real. I also told Jesus that I was sorry for my

---

58 Martin and I were married a few years later.

sins, and I asked Him to save me, but I will tell you honestly that I didn't fully understand what this meant. At that time, I didn't believe in life after death, so the gospel didn't really make sense to me. I just knew this was what Christians were supposed to do. I didn't figure out what it really meant until several years later.

Three things happened almost immediately after that morning. The first was that I was given, as a gift, the ability to trust God. This is quite remarkable given that I wasn't even sure that He existed, but I found that I was able to trust Him completely—to walk through each day with the certainty that God was guiding me and would take me where I needed to go, even though I didn't know where that was or how to get there. Trusting God each day and leaning on Him felt like coming home. I suppose this was part of what it meant for me to live my life as if God existed. I would trust Him. The second thing that happened was that I discovered to my delight that God didn't swallow me or squash me. Instead, I felt even more free than I had before. The third thing that happened was that people around me began to comment that I had changed—that I seemed different, nicer. Curious! I didn't feel any different. What was it that other people were noticing? When I thought about it, I began to realize that what had changed were my desires. I wanted to know God, to walk with Him each day, to trust Him, and I didn't care nearly as much about my own dignity. I am not sure whether or not this is what other people were noticing, but they were at least right that God was changing me from the inside out.

Here I need to backtrack once again and fill in a few details. Martin and I had been friends for a couple of years by this time, and for Christmas that year, Martin had given me a New English New Testament. It was small enough for me to carry around campus, and I set about attempting to read it right away. But I ran into a snag. You see, words are not just dictionary definitions. They also come with all kinds of emotional baggage depending on our previous experience. So for example, if you heard me say the word "Thanksgiving," you probably wouldn't just think of the dictionary definition, "The national holiday celebrated on the fourth Thursday of November . . . ." No, instead what would go through your mind would be a kaleidoscope of thoughts and feelings associated with all the many Thanksgiving holidays you have experienced in your life—the smell of roasted turkey and pumpkin pie, the warmth of family love, or the distress of family discord, short fall days, crispness in the air, falling leaves, and so forth. All of that would flash through your mind in an instant and add a great deal of emotional color to the word. That is how language works, and of course that is also why foreign languages lack color when we are first learning them. The new words haven't yet acquired an emotional history.

The problem I had when I read the New Testament was that, even though I came from a very loving family, I still had no models for the kind of self-sacrificing, altruistic love that Jesus exhibited. As a consequence, a number of the stories I read brought emotional images to my mind that were actually quite ugly. For example, many times in the gospels Jesus is referred to as "master" by the disciples. That word brought an ugly emotional picture to my mind. The image I got was of a mean school teacher who peered down her nose at you, waggled her finger, and said, "I am doing this for your own good," when you knew she didn't care one wit about you. It also brought images of the ugly heritage of slavery we have in this country. Not good stuff! Most of this was pretty subliminal. I was only semi-aware of what was happening, but I couldn't read more than a few paragraphs of the Bible before it made me feel almost physically sick. I was intrigued but also sickened, and I would hastily put the Bible away, only to take it out again a few hours later to read a few more paragraphs. I am bothering to tell you this because most Christians are so used to dwelling in the light of God's goodness that we don't realize how the Bible might appear to someone who is truly on the outside, reading it for the first time. There is also the very real problem of spiritual warfare. I am sure the devil was not at all happy with my reading attempts and was doing his level best to make the Bible seem unpalatable.

I had read through nearly all of the New Testament by the time I began my experiment to discover if God existed, but I can tell you honestly that I didn't understand most of it. I simply had no models in my previous life for making sense of what I read, and many wrong emotional pictures and impressions to blind me to what it was really all about. I am very grateful that Jesus was not stopped by any of this. He drew me gently to Himself in spite of it, and very patiently began the arduous task of untangling and dismantling all my wrong thoughts and emotional pictures.

So what happened to my experiment? It took about three years of living as a Christian before I felt that I could see the world through Christian eyes and compare my two worldviews side by side. When I did, God won easily. There was no going back. A world with God at its center made everything clearer, just like that fuzzy blob in the distance, and it was also vastly more colorful and warm.

Why? Just what is wrong with the agnostic worldview I grew up with? Such a big and difficult question. I can answer it, but not in a few words. The only simple thing I can say is that there is evidence for the existence of God. Much of that evidence is subjective and experiential. That is why it would take a lot of words to explain. There is no one experience, no one story that I could point to and say, "This one thing convinces me that there is a God." There is only a sum total, 41 years' worth of stories and consistent experiences that convince me.

One thing I discovered was that the evolutionary theory of religion I grew up with—the idea that religion is something humans made up to help them cope with life—simply isn't big enough to explain either Christianity or God. That idea is what religion looks like from the outside and from far away. It is like looking at a chain of mountains on the horizon. From far away, they look almost as if they could be made of purple cardboard, cut out with a pair of scissors and stacked one behind the other. But when you get up close it is another matter altogether, and when you are right in among them, they are anything but paper and cardboard. There are more and more wondrous valleys and hidden meadows to explore, and the cardboard cutout theory is just too simplistic. It sounds nice and very logical, as long as you are far away and don't look too closely, but it just doesn't hold water once you are actually in among the mountains and hills.

I used to imagine that God was like an invisible pillar in the middle of a room. Before I crossed the line from agnosticism to theism, I was walking all around this invisible pillar like a good scientist trying to determine if it existed. I had all my instruments with me and was very busy measuring air pressure and temperature, trying to see if there was anything different about the way light was scattered around the room, but none of these attempts got me anywhere. Finally one day, I walked boldly to the center of the room and leaned on the pillar. To my great surprise I discovered that when I pushed on the pillar, *it pushed back*. When I leaned on it, I didn't fall on my face. And not only that, but people around me who had tried the same experiment had gotten the same result. A subjective result, yes, but not necessarily invalid, and perhaps the best we can do when it comes to answering a question that is beyond the realm of science.

When I first began to live as if God existed, I gradually discovered things that did not fit within my previous agnostic model of world. They were things like answered prayer, odd coincidences, spiritual experiences, God's voice speaking to me, words of knowledge, prophecy, and miracles.

If you have ever gone through the exercise of choosing what color to repaint your house, you will remember that you suddenly became aware of the colors of all the other houses in your neighborhood. Whereas before when you walked around the neighborhood you were more or less oblivious to the colors of the houses around you, now you noticed everything. Here is another example: Have you ever tried to paint a picture that included the corner of a room? We all know walls are usually painted the same color on either side of a corner, but if you use the same color in your painting, the corner will be invisible. If you notice that one wall is shaded more than the other and paint one a darker color, the corner will start to look like a corner, but it still won't look quite right. Look closer still. You can often see a faint white line running down the center of the corner and sometimes a darker line right next to it. Including these lines in your painting will finally make the corner look correct.

What we notice in the world around us has a lot to do with what we focus on. We tend not to see things that aren't relevant to whatever we are doing, so most of the time we don't notice how light bounces around in the corner of a room. We don't notice until we try to paint it, and then suddenly we are forced to take a much closer look. When I was living as an agnostic, I hadn't noticed any evidence for the existence of God precisely because I wasn't looking for it. When I started living as if God existed, I began to notice spiritual things that didn't fit within my agnostic model of the world. Some of these things had been around me all the time, but I hadn't *seen* them, or if I *had* seen them, I had unconsciously dismissed them, since they didn't fit within my current worldview. They had been like all the house colors in the neighborhood that I never noticed, or the light and dark lines running down the center of the corner of a room that I didn't realize were there until I took the time to look. Now I began to pay attention to these things, wonder about them, and try to figure them out.

Science is like this. It tends to move forward in giant leaps which we call paradigm shifts. In my own field of geology, plate tectonics (the notion that the Earth's crust is divided into moving plates) took more than 500 years to be accepted. The idea of continental drift was first suggested in 1596 by a cartographer called Abraham Ortelius, who noticed the remarkable geometric fit of the coastline of South America with that of Africa. Later scientists noticed matching rock and fossil sequences in the mountain ranges on either side of the ocean. Alfred Wegener proposed a more fully developed version of the theory in 1912. By 1950, impressive lines of evidence were piling up in its favor, including rock-magnetic data showing that either the continents or the Earth's polar ice cap had moved. Nevertheless, the theory of plate tectonics was not widely accepted and was often ridiculed. In the 1960's, the discovery of magnetic reversal stripes on the seafloor and patterns of earthquakes around the globe made the evidence for plate tectonics so overwhelming that the theory was finally accepted. Why did it take so long? Because the earlier theory of mountain building was so firmly entrenched and widely believed that data contradicting it tended to be either dismissed or ignored. That is how we humans work. We don't like having our models of the world messed with. We much prefer the stability of continuing as we always have, and we will go to great lengths to squeeze contrary data into our current model—somehow—as long as we possibly can. That is what happened to me. I was dismissing spiritual experiences as either coincidences or "bad data," and I wasn't focusing my attention on God. This led me to believe that there wasn't any evidence for God's existence, even though that evidence is actually not all that unusual or uncommon.

It has now been 41 years since I gave my life to God and started living as if He existed, and I have never regretted this decision or wanted to go back to living as an agnostic. Accepting spiritual experiences, answered prayer, miracles, and God's voice in my life as *real* completely changed the way I saw and interacted with everything. It turned my previous understanding of the world upside down. Giving my life to Jesus put everything in its proper place. It made the world warm and lovely. It gave me room to breathe. It made sense of the spiritual experiences I had previously been dismissing. It made life worth living. It filled me with love for everything and made me want to spend my life caring for others. It made me feel worthwhile, accepted, and forgiven. I was like a bud opening up to be a flower, or an egg hatching out to be a baby chick. Who would ever want to go back, to voluntarily live again within the cramped confining spaces of a bud or an egg shell? Definitely not me!

Here are some examples of experiences that I once dismissed but now accept as evidence for the reality of God.

Answered prayer happens frequently. For example, I almost can't count the number of times I have spent hours hunting for some lost object only to finally remember, "Oh, I should pray about this," after which I find the lost item within five minutes. Of course it is impossible to know what would have happened if I hadn't prayed. Also, there *are* times when my prayers just seem to bounce off the ceiling, with every answer being either "no" or silence. Prayer is an elusive thing to study objectively. Nevertheless, God answers prayer. Here are a few examples:

When Martin and I were living in Texas, back in the 1980's, we met a woman named Susan who lived in our neighborhood. Susan was a brand new Christian still getting it all figured out. She was also using illegal drugs. Martin felt that since she was a new Christian, we should go over to her house and talk to her about her drug use, and he wanted me to come with him. Now, confronting people is something I do *not* like to do—not at all. The very thought completely terrified me, but I agreed to go with him. To shorten the story, we did talk with Susan, she decided to get rid of her drugs, and we helped her. When this was finished, we stood in a circle, put our hands on each others' shoulders, and prayed that God would bless Susan's new Christian life. When I touched Susan's shoulder, I felt what seemed like a bolt of electricity coming out of my hand and going into her shoulder. She felt it too, and turned to stare at me. She said that the bolt of electricity came from my hand, traveled all the way down her side, and left through her foot on the floor. Only twice have I had this experience of electricity strongly flowing through me during prayer. I have learned from my experience and from others who have felt the same thing, that when this happens in prayer, God often answers with a special kind of clarity and power. To my knowledge, Susan never used drugs again and her life changed in ways that made her a happier person.

The other time I experienced electricity flowing through me in prayer was when I prayed for healing for a woman named Nancy (not my sister) who was in a Bible study we attended when we lived in England. She was healed.

A different kind of answer to prayer happened once when we were facing a difficult medical decision. It was a trying situation and we didn't know what to do. I disappeared into the next room to pray. Not more than five minutes later the phone rang, and it was one of only two people we personally knew who had the life experience necessary to advise us about this decision. What is remarkable is that we have known this person for something like 35 years, and that was the only time he has ever called us on the phone. Plus, it was a long-distance call from another state, which was costly in those days. This was also the only time in the last 35 years that we have faced a decision he was uniquely qualified to weigh in on. How many days are there in 35 years? Around 12,780. Could this have been a coincidence? Yes. Was it a coincidence? I doubt it.

Here is a different kind of story. When I first began reading the New Testament, I read a number of things that were challenging, but since Jesus said to do them, I tried to obey. One of the things I read was about letting go of anger and forgiving the people around you. It greatly surprises me that I was so slow to learn this, but for some reason up until that time it had never occurred to me that I didn't have to get angry if someone did something I didn't like. What! You mean I actually have a choice? I practiced letting go of resentment and anger, and as a consequence discovered the relaxing sweetness that comes from being at peace with myself and my world. Wow!

Could I have learned this from some other source than the Bible? Yes, certainly. There are atheists who are better at this than some Christians. But *I* learned these things by reading Jesus' words and attempting to put them into practice. I learned that the advice for living I found in the Bible was good, and worth following.

❧

Here is a story about "words of knowledge" and the ability to discern spirits. The Bible talks about Christians being given spiritual gifts for the edification of the church, and one of these gifts is the ability to know something about another person, that from a human point of view, you had no natural way of learning.

One day, when I was a new graduate student, I had not been able to sleep the night before, and I was feeling very crabby and tired. As a consequence, I attempted to take a nap on the couch in the graduate student lounge. I was still a new student, and I knew very few of the other students (there were around 100 in that department). I had never told anyone that I was a Christian, and if there were other Christians in that department, I had not yet met any of them.

A woman I had never seen before walked into the graduate student lounge. She looked around the room, which had four people in it, none of whom I knew, and said brightly, "Only three dead people in here today." Then she turned and looked at me intently. I looked back, wondering what the weird statement she had just made could possibly mean. She continued staring at me and said slowly, "No, there are only two dead people in here today." Then she smiled at me and sat down in a chair to start her homework. What! Something in me understood that she knew I was a Christian, even though I had never told anyone, and even though I thought my crabby tired soul was a pretty poor example of Christianity at that particular moment. I later found out that she was slightly autistic and a bit socially challenged, which at least partially explains her unusual communication style. I also had the chance to test her skills on someone she had not yet met whom I had discovered was a Christian. She was right, and she was also right about every other Christian I met in that department during the several years I spent there.

This woman had the gift of "discerning spirits." What was she seeing? Christians would say that she was seeing the Holy Spirit, who takes up residence within every Christian when they give their life to God.

Here is a story about strange spiritual beings. This happened in Oklahoma when we were in the process of packing up the house and getting ready to move to Nebraska.

In the final few days that we lived in that house, the landlord brought around a young couple who were thinking about renting the place after we left. They seemed like a perfectly ordinary, nice young couple, but after they came to visit, strange things began happening in the house. The next morning, when I was outside hanging up laundry and Martin was in bed asleep, our little electric kitchen radio suddenly turned on, very loudly, to a station we never listened to. It was an old fashioned radio with a dial you had to turn to set the station. There were no push buttons or remote control. We never listened to anything but classical music at a moderate volume, but this was a pop station turned up very loud. I rushed into the kitchen from the garden to turn it off, but it felt so weird. How could something like that happen? How does a radio just spontaneously turn itself on and self-adjust the station and volume? Later that afternoon the young couple came around because they wanted to buy our refrigerator, so I asked them if they had signed a lease for the house. They had signed the lease that morning, right about the time the radio went crazy in our kitchen.

Two days later the movers came to take away our stuff, and after that we were left in a nearly empty house with only the few things we planned to take with us in the car. We intended to spend that day cleaning, camp in the house overnight, and leave the following morning. But that day another weird thing happened. Because our tea kettle was packed and gone, I tried to heat water for tea in a small saucepan. I turned on the electric stove, put the water on to heat, and turned my attention to cleaning something on the other side of the kitchen. Suddenly, the water exploded out of the pan, splashing all over the room. When I went to investigate, the pan was still sitting on the stove, with very little water left in it. (This was right next to where the radio had been two days earlier.) What could that possibly mean? I have asked several physicists how this could happen. Most have told me they had no idea, but one told me that the water had to somehow become super-heated, as could possibly happen if there was oil on top of it. Since I was curious, I tried duplicating this scenario by intentionally putting oil on heating water, but all that happened was that the water came to a boil in a totally normal way. Besides, on the day this happened I was heating perfectly ordinary water for tea, not water with oil on top, and the water had not yet come to a boil.

It felt to me as if "someone" had moved into the house, someone with a mischievous temperament who enjoyed playing tricks. It was creepy—so creepy that we changed our plans and left early. I felt comfortable staying in the house as long as it was legally ours, but I didn't feel comfortable camping overnight and leaving the next morning, which was the first day of the next month. I just didn't want to find out what this mischievous spirit might do when the house was no longer legally ours. So at around nine-thirty that evening we piled our sleepy kids in the car, drove an hour up the road, and crashed overnight in a motel.

There are other stories of encounters with the unholy spirit that I could tell, but this one is the most straightforward.

The final area of evidence for God I should mention is simple Christian apologetics. There are a lot of well-researched books dealing with the historical evidence for what is written in the New Testament, and some of these books are quite good. I have read a number of them, and they have convinced me that the historical evidence for Christianity is remarkably solid. For some examples see: *Evidence that Demands a Verdict* by Josh McDowell, *Letters from a Skeptic* by Gregory Boyd, or *Who Moved the Stone* by Frank Morison.

If you work hard enough, and especially if you don't pay too much attention to detail, you can probably find some excuse for dismissing, or explaining away, any one of these stories. But the sum total of them is not so easily dismissed, especially when you add my experiences together with those of Martin, my sister Nancy, and every other Christian I personally know.

The stories I have shared are just a tiny sample. When I first started living as if God was real, these sorts of experiences stood out because they didn't fit comfortably within my previous agnostic worldview. For maybe three to ten years, I was able to hold the agnostic worldview and the Christian worldview in my head side by side and compare them. But now that it has been 41 years, I can no longer see the "God does not exist" worldview from the inside. It is too remote and hard to remember. Now when I lie out under the stars at night and think of the vastness and complexity of the universe, just the sheer energy of it all, it seems to me ludicrous that anyone could think that the universe came into existence without some kind of intelligence behind it. But once that idea seemed rational and normal to me.

My switch to a completely Christian view of the world also means that experiences such as I have just described no longer jar me. They have become normal, so I often don't even think about trying to remember them, or about writing them down. They are like the colors of houses in my neighborhood that I tend not to notice. When these things happen, I just thank God for His care and move on with my life. But I have written down these few examples for the sake of you, my reader, because I have found that a life with Jesus at its center is a beautiful and full life, and one that is well worth living.

A Meditation on Philippians 4:8

Barbara Gaskell

All that is true, all that is honorable,
All that is right, all that is pure,
Whatever is lovely, gracious and excellent,
Anything worthy of praise,
Let your mind dwell on these things.

God's Holy word forever reliable,
Peace in our hearts, hope in our souls,
Forgiveness and mercy for all of our foolishness,
Jesus our savior adored,
Let your mind dwell on these things.

. . . .

Servants of God, living in harmony,
Families who love, neighbors who care,
Saints who have gone before us in faithfulness,
Friends who are faithful in prayer,
Let your mind dwell on these things.

God's wondrous world, astounding and intricate,
Showing God's might, beauty and love,
From crickets and pine cones to lightning and hurricanes,
God's power and wisdom are known,
Let your mind dwell on these things.

Sunshine and dew, owls and fireflies,
Green leaves and oaks, clattering hail,
With beauty around us and love to encourage us,
Our hope and joy will not fail,
Let your mind dwell on these things.

All that is true, all that is honorable,
All that is right, all that is pure,
Whatever is lovely, gracious and excellent,
Anything worthy of praise,
Let your mind dwell on these things.

A Meditation on Philippians 4:8

Barbara Gaskell

Mercy Triumphs Over Judgment

Barbara Gaskell

Verses

27
G C Am C G

Not | many of | us | are | migh – ty | or | no – ble,
How | ma – ny | times | must | I – | for – | give,
Why | do you | judge | a – no – | ther's | ser – vant.
Do – | not re – | turn | e – vil | for | e – vil

32
C D G Am

most | of | us | are | weak. | But | God chose | us | to
up | to | se – ven | times? | Not | se – ven | times, but
Who | do, you | thin – k you | are? | Be – | fore his, own | mas – ter
Give | a | bles – sing in – stead. | En – | cour-age, the | fai – nt

38
G D G G Am D

bri – ng Him | glor – y, | to | be | His | hand | and | feet,
seven – ty times | sev – en, | seventy | times | sev – en | times.
he – | will | sta – nd | He | will | sta – nd or | fall.
he – lp | the | we – ak | be | pa – tient | wi – th all | men.

43
Am D G D G

to | shine like | stars, | to in – her – it a | king-dom, but | still
Have | mer – cy | on | your | fel – low | men | for | God
But | God | is | a – ble to | ma – ke him | sta – nd | for | God
No | eye has | seen, | nor | ear | has | hea – rd what | God

49
C F D G C C G G D

be, | still | be, | still | be | hum-ble and | mee – k. | Mer – cy
has, | God | has, | God | has | mer – cy | on | you.
is, | God | is, | God | is | ov – er | all.
has, | God | has, | God | has | wait-ing for | you.

57
G C D Am G Am G

tri – umphs | ov – ver | ju – dg – ment.

O LORD, our Lord,
How majestic is Your name in all the earth,
Who have displayed Your splendor above the heavens!
When I consider Your heavens, the work of Your
　　　fingers,
The moon and the stars, which You have ordained;
What is man that You take thought of him,
And the son of man that You care for him?

Psalm 8, verses 1, 3, & 4 (NASB)

The Heavens Declare
The Glory of God

Martin Gaskell

When people find out that I'm both an astrophysicist and a Christian, they sometimes ask whether I became a Christian before or after I became an astronomer. My conversion was actually an indirect by-product of the path to becoming an astronomer. However, the early steps of that path are ones you should *not* follow! So when I explain what happened I have to say, "Don't try this at home!" At times I've been reluctant to tell the story, thinking that for many people it might sound unusual and surely not relevant. However, I have now had not one but *two* astronomers ask me how I became a Christian and then, to my immense surprise, after hearing my story, tell me that *they* had done very similar things with similar outcomes!

I am someone who knew from an early age what I wanted to do, and I've been blessed by being able to spend my life doing it. I was born in England. When I was in the British equivalent of kindergarten or first grade, there was a nice lady who watched over us during lunch recess. One lunch time she asked me and the other little kids what we wanted to be when we grew up. I still remember replying with no hesitation, "A scientist!" A couple of years later I read some of my cousin's astronomy books, and I was hooked. I asked for, and was given, a telescope for my 10th birthday, and by the time I was 11, I was earning extra money to build a much bigger telescope. My interest in astronomy led to a strong interest in mathematics and physics in school, and before I knew it, I was set on the course that led to where I am now.

Even at that fairly young age (11 going on 12), I pondered big ultimate questions such as, "Is the universe infinite?" "Did the universe have a beginning?" or, "What is the ultimate nature of matter?" I've always been a "do-it-myself" person, so it is my nature to be most excited by things I can research and explore myself. Because I could build my own telescopes, while I could not build my own particle accelerator, astronomy was the clear choice for me. (Interestingly, I have subsequently met not one but two physicists who actually *did* build their own particle accelerators in high school! One blew out the power in his entire neighborhood when he turned it on!) The only other career direction I gave fleeting consideration to was going into music.

One Christmas or birthday, when I was 11 or 12, a relative gave me a science book. It had three types of content. The first was straight-forward science—this was what I really wanted to read. Then there was science fiction. That was OK. Like many scientists I had an early passing interest in science fiction. I lost interest though when I found the realities of science *fact* to be *much* more interesting than the obviously unrealistic speculations of science fiction. (Surely nobody would ever have a radio telephone they could hide in the palm of their hand!) The separation between science fact and science fiction was very clear to me, so there was no confusion. However, there was a *third* component to that book—what I would now call "pseudo-science." The book described experiments in what is called "extra-sensory perception," or "ESP" for short. The experiments seemed innocuous enough. What interested me was that they were simple experiments I could do myself and, as I've said, I've always been a "do-it-myself" person. At this time I was not spiritually searching, but it was obvious that these ESP experiments could be a way of demonstrating in a supposedly scientific way whether the supernatural existed. I won't describe the experiments except to say that they were about whether one could learn information outside of the usual sensory channels, and whether by the same means one could influence things. The outcome was that I thought I was getting positive results. I was finding that there *was* a supernatural!

One might think that it is an exciting and positive experience to be finding that there is a supernatural, but that was not the case: It was *not* a good experience. The best way I can describe what happened is that it was like the classic fairy tale where a beautiful young woman marries a strange man in a castle (for example, as in the old French folk tale "Bluebeard"). She is told she can do anything she wants and go anywhere she pleases in the castle except for one locked room. Well, human nature being what it is, sooner or later the young woman unlocks the forbidden door and looks inside the room. She has then opened up some dark evil and there is no going back. That describes my experience well, although nobody had told me not to do what I was doing. I didn't like what I was getting into, but I kept going. I thought that I could gain some higher knowledge about the universe. I started doing experiments to see if I could telepathically get people to do little things, innocent things like scratch the back of their neck, for example. Again, I thought I was getting positive results.

This was taking place in 1965 going into early 1966. The mid-1960's were tumultuous times with the rise of the "counterculture" as it was then called. This almost entirely passed by the town where I lived, but there were some inevitable influences. The Maharishi Mahesh Yogi from India had been to Britain. He had been publishing about the *Bhagavad Gita* around 1963–64 and was lecturing about Transcendental Meditation. A few years later he was to rise to higher celebrity status when the Beatles visited him, but that lay in the future. The Maharishi taught about how he thought yoga could raise consciousness to a higher level. I don't remember where or how I heard these ideas. What I do know is that one day (probably in late 1965 or early 1966), I was sitting in the sandbox of the long jump on the far side of the school playing field during the lunchtime recess. My legs were crossed in a yoga position, I had my eyes closed, and I was trying (with no success) to gain "higher consciousness" knowledge of the universe. I was now 12 years old. Because I had my eyes closed, and because of the noise of children in the playing field, I did not hear the approach of two bratty girls in the year below mine. They surprised me and taunted me in a sing-song sort of way, saying, "What are *you* doing? Are you *praying*?" I opened my eyes abruptly and quickly responded, "No, I am not *praying*, I am *meditating*." To me at the time, prayer was just something people did in church, something I was not going to get caught doing at school during lunchtime! I thought that the proper "modern" thing to do was to "meditate." However, as the girls were going away and I was thinking about going back to my "meditating," something inside me, or rather some*body*—somebody who I would now recognize as the Holy Spirit—said in a calm way, "But you *should* have been praying."

Despite this little incident, I kept up my supernatural quest. However, the problems got worse. What I was quite unaware of at the time was that I was doing things God expressly forbids in the Bible. Although I would not have used this terminology then, what I was doing was what the Bible calls "divination" (trying to gain knowledge supernaturally and foretell the future) and "sorcery" (trying to influence or control things or events supernaturally). I was getting into the realm of what the Bible calls demons. All this was very scary for a 12-year old boy. At the time, of course, I didn't use the word "demons," but I was becoming aware that my ESP experiments and "meditation" were leading me *not* to some cosmic force or the solution to a cosmic mystery, but to something personal, or more accurately, some *things* that were personal. It seemed that they were "after me" and I became quite afraid. In particular I became afraid of the dark. There were two problems with that. The first was that my hobby was astronomy, and you have to go outside in the dark to see stars and planets through a telescope. I remember that I solved that problem, around Christmas time 1965, by looking through an open upper window from inside the house! I also arranged for one of my best friends to go stargazing with me on the lawn outside. It was still a little scary even with him there. The second problem was that I was a boy, and boys are not supposed to be afraid of the dark!

Not too long after this (I think it was in February), what I can now call the demonic presence and threats were getting progressively more and more frightening. As I often did at the time, I thought about things as I paced around the school playing field at lunchtime. I was by some tall poplar trees near the iron railings across the road from the school. It was a gray, cold, but dry wintery day. I was thinking about what was going on demonically. Night time was particularly scary, but things had become bad enough that I was now not even comfortable at school in the day time. I was thinking about what I would face back at home when night came. As I was in the middle of contemplating this, suddenly, out of the blue, something happened. The simplest way to explain it is to say that God spoke to me.

At this point one can reasonably ask, "What do you mean by 'God spoke to you'? Was there an audible voice?" The answer is, no, it was not an audible external voice. It was just God clearly speaking inside me. It was a male voice with a neutral accent (at the time it would therefore have been a British English accent). It was the same voice that had told me in the sandbox that I should be praying. When I explain this, some people are curious and ask more questions while others say, "Yes, I know just what you mean."

What the voice said to me was, "You should be following My Son, Jesus. In Him there is perfect safety." Jesus was not someone I had thought about at all in my supernatural searching. He was someone who I had filed away in my brain in the unexciting category of "church," a place where people prayed, something I had emphatically told those girls at the sandbox that I was *not* doing. I had certainly heard the title, "Jesus, the Son of God," but it had meant little to me; certainly not that He really *was* the Son of God. In fact, God didn't figure in my view of the universe up until that point either. For me the question had been, "Is there a supernatural?" not, "Is there a God?" Given the apparently positive results of my ESP experiments and the obvious reality of the demonic realms, I could not intellectually argue that a supernatural God could not, or did not, exist, but I had not seriously thought about Him yet. All that changed in a flash with Him speaking to me.

At the time, I did not know the verse in Proverbs about the Lord being a strong tower that I could flee to: "The name of the LORD is a strong tower; the righteous runs into it and is safe." Proverbs 18:10 (New American Standard Bible) But that describes very well what God was conveying to me. I was immediately aware that God, who was speaking to me, was vastly more powerful than the demonic realms I had been getting into. I had no choice but to respond. I therefore said inwardly to Him, "Yes, Lord, I'm going to follow Your Son Jesus for the rest of my life." As soon as I said that, all the demonic oppression immediately went away. That evening, I don't think even the thought that there could be demonic activity and threats occurred to me. I was never afraid of the dark again. Indeed, since then I have always found the dark comforting, as it is quiet and one gets to see farther out into God's universe.

Going back to my ESP experiments, I should explain why I say "I thought" I was getting positive results. There are two reasons. The first is that the results would most likely not have stood up to a rigorous statistical analysis, had I then been capable of doing such analyses. The second reason is that the Bible says Satan is "the father of lies" (John 8:44b, NASB), so I was undoubtedly being deceived.

God conveyed two other things to me that lunchtime in the school playing field: First, I should pray to Him daily, and second, I should start reading the Bible daily. At that stage I believe I had read the Bible from Genesis chapter 1 all the way to . . . Genesis chapter 2! (I was interested in the question of cosmic origins, so I wanted to see what Genesis had to say.) I now began reading the New Testament. I started praying that evening, and I have maintained a pattern of daily prayer ever since. I did not realize it until many years later, but after I said "yes" to Jesus, God took away all of my curiosity about ESP.

Not only did God instantaneously take away the demonic oppression and my fear, but He changed my attitudes. As I think back now, I can see that many changes were made in me. One that stands out was my attitude towards church. I had thought that people who went to church were hypocrites. I actually had no evidence whatsoever that they really were—I had either made the idea up myself or, more likely, picked it up from school. My attitude changed immediately, and I never saw church goers as hypocrites again. Something that has always been clear to me is the vital necessity of regular church attendance. My career has taken me to remote countries, and wherever I am, I try without fail to gather with other Christians on Sunday, even if I don't understand the language they are speaking.

No great spiritual growth occurred during my high school years, nor during my undergraduate years until near the end. At university, Christians were more obvious than they had been in high school (I don't think I knew a single other Christian in high school). I noticed at university that there were some Christians who were better Christians than I was. Three things about them stood out. First, they were very serious about the Bible, more so than I was then. Were they being *too* serious about it, I wondered? But when I thought about this, I realized that very close to 100 percent of what we know about Jesus is in the Bible, so if one is to be serious about following Jesus, one has to be serious about studying the Bible. That made sense. The second thing was that these Christians prayed a lot more than I did, and the third thing was that they spoke about answers to prayer— things seemed to happen around them.

An important day in my life was one Saturday morning in the middle of my last year as an undergraduate. This was at the University of Edinburgh in Scotland. Some students from the British equivalent of InterVarsity Christian Fellowship were going door to door in my residence hall. "Hello! We're a bunch of Christians, and we're inviting people to attend Bible studies," they said after knocking on my door. I immediately thought, 'I'm a Christian! I ought to go to a Bible study group!' So I accepted their invitation and started attending a weekly Bible study in a student's room in a nearby residence hall. For the first time I was in an environment where the Bible was really being studied. I also got to experience the warmth of relationships among Christians in a small group for the first time. I mentioned above that I had noticed that more mature Christians prayed a lot. In fact, they prayed so much and so long at the end of these Bible studies that I remember getting impatient. I also remember on at least one occasion getting back to my own room and asking God's forgiveness for that impatience! Needless to say, my attitude towards time spent in prayer soon changed.

After I graduated I entered the doctoral program in astrophysics at the University of California in Santa Cruz (UCSC). Within a week I met other Christian graduate students. I now knew the importance of small groups and Bible study, so I got involved in the Christian graduate student fellowship. Also, for the first time in my life, I attended a church where the teaching was thoroughly centered on the Bible. After or between services, rather than merely talking about the weather (the standard British thing to do!), people were talking about what God had shown them in scripture that week. They were asking each other to pray for needs, and they were reporting back answers to prayers. The result of the enormously positive influence of this church and the Christian graduate student fellowship was that by the time I finished my PhD, I was spending far more time in Bible study. I realized that the Bible was a book with answers, practical answers. I was praying far more as well, and I too was beginning to see remarkable answers to prayer. The Bible says, "Draw near to God and He will draw near to you." James 4:8a (NASB)

A common misconception is that scientists are a bunch of atheists. Many people are surprised when surveys of scientists' beliefs show that, in fact, atheists are a minority. For people interested in this, a useful place to go is the book *Science vs. Religion: What Scientists Really Think* (Oxford University Press, 2010) by Rice University social science professor Elaine Howard Ecklund. She surveyed 1,646 scientists (physicists, chemists, and biologists) and social scientists. Her results are consistent with other surveys, but what makes her study particularly valuable is that she conducted open-ended, follow-up interviews with a random subset of 275 of the respondents. From this one learns that only five of the scientists she interviewed were actively working against religion. Her interviews reveal, among other things, that for *scientists* who are non-believers, their reasons for non-belief are *similar* to the reasons of *non-scientists*. To quote Professor Eklund (see p. 17 of her book), ". . . for the majority of scientists [that she interviewed] it is *not the engagement with science itself that leads them away from religion*."[59]

Scientists' reasons for non-belief include: not having heard the Christian message, not thinking that faith is relevant to them, having had bad experiences with churches, and God not doing things the way they think He ought to. Once my wife and I took a non-Christian graduate-student friend to our large home Bible study group. The group mostly consisted of a mixture of university people (faculty, post-docs, and graduate students). We went around the circle introducing ourselves to our visitor. Our friend whispered in my ear, "It seems like most Christians are scientists! Where are people from the humanities?" "Oh," I whispered back, "They think being a Christian is unscientific!"

---

59 Italics added here for emphasis.

A question I am asked from time to time (more often by Christians than non-Christians) is what challenges do I struggle with between science and being a Christian. The short answer is that I don't. I think I'm quite typical in this regard. I've known many scientists who are Christians, and we've had many discussions individually, online, and as part of meetings (for example, we have a Christian astronomers group that meets at the national meetings of the American Astronomical Society). Struggles between faith and science are not a topic that comes up. My own view of my astronomical research is that I am learning new things about God's creation in so far as He allows. As I (imperfectly) learn about how God does things, I try to remember to thank Him for His gift of these insights. There are certainly mysteries and things we don't understand, but that is what keeps science going.

How does being a Christian influence how one does science? One way it ought to is in our attitudes and in the human interactions that are a large part of the scientific process. For example, a Christian should not treat a graduate student as a mere research slave whose only value is in the research he or she produces. Another way a Christian's worldview ought to influence his or her scientific activities is in a scrupulous concern for truth. There should not be compromises to advance the careers of oneself or one's students or to try to obtain more research funding. The Creator and sustainer of the universe knows far more about how His universe works than we ever will, and a scientist who is a Christian has a Heavenly Father who will take care of the scientist's career and research funding.

There are various misconceptions about Christians. One is that Christianity is just a convenient belief system or philosophy. But God did not only work in miraculous ways in the past (as

recorded, for example, in the *Acts of the Apostles* in the Bible);
He can answer prayer in miraculous ways today. If you talk with
Christians, you will hear stories of God working in miraculous,
supernatural ways. I don't think we talk enough about these.
Many times Barbara and I have experienced God at work in
remarkable ways. As an illustration I want to end with just a
couple of stories. I've picked these particular stories because I
can tell them without violating privacy. I've just changed names
and omitted identifying details.

Once, Barbara and I were in a church home group. There
were about a dozen of us. We were mostly science and
engineering types. (One housewife joked that she was a
"domestic engineer"!) We would sing hymns and Christian songs
together, study a passage from the Bible, and then go around the
circle to share prayer requests. After that, we would take time to
pray about each request. There was a woman in the group who
suffered from bad allergies. I will call her Jane (not her real
name). One week as Barbara and I were preparing to go to the
group, God impressed upon me that we should lay hands on Jane,
and pray for healing. I must explain that this was not something
the group had done before. I told Barbara what I thought God
was telling me, and Barbara said that God was telling her the
same thing. In fact, Barbara said God made her hands tingle with
a desire to lay hands on Jane and pray for her healing.

Off we went to the group, determined that we would
propose to lay hands on Jane and pray for her, even though this
was something the group had never done before. Our meeting
went the same as in previous weeks until the time came when we
normally went around the circle sharing prayer requests. To our
surprise, the leader of the group said, "Tonight, rather than

everybody sharing prayer requests, I think we should just pray for Jane."

Wow! Given the experience that Barbara and I had at home beforehand, and given what the group leader was now saying, God was clearly up to something! We listened attentively while Jane shared that she had received double bad news at the doctor's office that day. First, she had been diagnosed with breast cancer. Then the doctor told her she needed a hysterectomy (for an unrelated problem). When Jane had finished telling us this, Barbara and I had no hesitation in saying, "Jane, would it be OK if we laid hands on you and prayed for healing?" Jane and everyone else were in full agreement so we did.

What happened? The short answer is that God healed Jane. Given the circumstances, I would actually have been most surprised if God had *not* healed Jane. Each week Jane reported back to the group on her doctors' visits. Finally, after a few months, Jane reported that the doctors now said there was nothing wrong with her and no surgeries were going to be needed! Had God gradually healed Jane over a period of a couple of months? Or had God healed Jane immediately when we laid hands on her and prayed, but it took awhile for the doctors to figure this out? We don't know.

Back in the early 1990's, Barbara and I were wrestling with the problem of what to do about a medicine that was causing serious unwanted side effects. There were two medicines involved and we didn't know whether the problem was caused by one or both. We spent well over an hour late on a Friday night talking about this. What did the labels on the medicines say? How did the side effects correlate with possible causes? What was the best course of action? It was a Friday night, and it wouldn't be possible to contact the doctor's office until Monday. We tried to figure out the answers as best we could, but based on the evidence we had, we just couldn't decide what to do. Then we did what we should have done in the first place: We prayed about the problem.

The question then was, how would God answer our prayers? Nothing happened that night. We went to sleep. There were no answers at all the next morning, nor in the afternoon, but in the evening after dinner, just a few minutes after Barbara had been praying again about the problem, our telephone rang. It was someone we knew, although not particularly well—someone who had never called us before—someone who lived in a totally different part of the country. I will call him Peter (not his real name). One thing I knew about Peter was that he could probably answer our questions about side effects. In fact, he was the only person we knew who might be able to answer them.

"Hello, this is Peter. How are you?" said the caller. Knowing Peter's medical knowledge, I didn't simply reply, "We're all doing fine, thank you." Instead I launched straight away into telling Peter about our medicine side effects question. He was able to confidently tell us what the cause was and what the solution was. Our problem was solved. God had answered our prayers.

After I had hung up at the end of this providential phone call, I realized that I had never found out *why* Peter had called! He had never called us before. It was a long-distance call and they were expensive in those days. What is more, in over a quarter of a century since then, Peter has never called us again! I saw Peter a couple of years later, and I told him about the remarkable timing of his long-distance call. I asked him why he had called. He said he had *no* idea. Of all the 10,000 plus days that we've known Peter, he just felt that he should telephone us that particular day!

The heavens are telling of the glory of God;
And their expanse is declaring the work of His hands.
Day to day pours forth speech,
And night to night reveals knowledge.
There is no speech, nor are there words;
Their voice is not heard.
Their line has gone out through all the earth,
And their utterances to the end of the world.

             Psalm 19:1-4 (NASB)

From his fullness we have all received,
grace upon grace.

John 1:16 (New Revised Standard Version)

Grace upon Grace

Teresa Mohamed

Firstly, my disclaimer: There is no way on earth that a few pages can accurately sum up one person's journey to God, but the following is one attempt.

"Questa e` una storia semplice." This is a simple story. "Eppure non e` facile raccontarla." And yet it is not easy to tell. "Come in una favola c'e` dolore." As in a fairy tale there is pain. "E come in una favola e` piena di meraviglie e di felicita." And as in a fairy tale it is full of wonders and happiness. (The first lines from the film *La Vita e` Bella* by Roberto Benigni)

My mother was in and out of mental hospitals basically my entire life. Her diagnosis was schizophrenic, paranoid. My mother's sickness was tragically intertwined with God and the Bible and sex. She believed she was mentioned in the Bible. She believed she was the Shulamite girl[60] and the Bride of Christ. As the years passed, she believed herself to be Jehovah God Himself. At any given time, she would shave her head and eyebrows completely. She took potato sacks and sewed a long dress of sackcloth using a rope for a belt. She donned these absurdities and placed ashes on her forehead as a kind of act of repentance. It was a horrible sight to see. Then on another day she might wear a long black curly wig, paint her face up with every bit of make up one might imagine, put on a flimsy dress of some sort, resembling what she would refer to as a "harlot," and walk the streets of Sacramento. A few times she just took

---

60 See: The Song of Solomon.

everything off and walked down the K Street Mall totally nude—bald head and all.

When she was off her medication, she did some very sick things to five very innocent children. I was the middle child.

As you can imagine, with a deranged out-of-control mother who had all her sickness wrapped up in the Bible and God, I rejected anything to do with God or religion, and I chose my atheist father as my most stable ally. Although he too had his own diagnosis of manic depression and was an alcoholic, he wasn't deranged or delusional. So I chose to be far away from religion, from the Bible, and from a God that at the time I didn't believe existed, and to stay as close as possible to my father.

Growing up, however, there was always this feeling inside —what I called my "sick empty feeling." I think it is what some refer to as that God-shaped hole inside that only He can fill.

Looking back now, I can see my coming to faith in very distinct ways, and yet the process was rather slow. But it happened! And I am so grateful for this gift of faith my God has given me.

When I was in college, I tutored a young, maybe 15-year-old girl who had decided she wanted to become a nun and join an order in Italy. At the time I thought she was out of her mind. Go to Italy and do what?!? During one of our tutoring sessions the phone rang at her house. She picked it up and explained that she was having an Italian tutoring session and couldn't talk. That girl radiated such joy. I remember that she had long, shiny black hair and bright brown eyes. As she got off the phone she said to the person on the other end, "OK, bye, God bless you!" I had never heard anyone say anything like that before. It really moved me. I suddenly wished she would say that to me! I didn't know why. I just wanted her to tell *me* that. I wanted to hear her say that to me too, "God bless you, Teresa." But she never did.

And then I met my husband, Thomas. I loved everything about him, except what he believed. Could I just have him without the God part? He would be perfect without this God thing. And we would argue—heated arguments. "Of course, God exists," he would say, and I would retort, "There is no way!" How could it be? What about all the suffering? My Dad used to say, "If there is a God, He's got one hell of a sense of humor." In Dostoevsky's *The Brothers Karamazov*—The Grand Inquisitor chapter—Ivan, the atheist brother, could accept it all but not the babies on the bayonets—that he could not accept. I wholeheartedly agreed with my Dad and yet, and yet, as Thomas spoke to me, deep down inside I just wished it were all true. Could it really be true? If only it were true. . . .

And then came the birth of my first son—Aaron. And the only word I could think to describe this was "a miracle." And miracle is a religious word, isn't it? With the birth of each child the same word came to me, "miracle." The gift of life. The gift of faith. The gift of love.

While living in Sacramento, I became friends with a lady who lived down the street, Debbie. She was an extraordinarily strong Christian and would talk to me about God, about Jesus, the Holy Spirit, and the Bible. I remember asking her just how one comes to faith, and she told me that it was like falling backwards and trusting you would be caught. But I was not ready to fall backwards at that point. I was not ready to surrender and give it all to Jesus.

We moved to Bonny Doon with our two boys and then had a third son—"My Three Sons"[61]—Aaron, Matty, and

---

61 An American sitcom that ran from 1960 through 1972.

Tommy. Our sweet neighbor, Helen, invited us to church, and we declined. Then she asked if she could pick up the boys and take them. We consented to this, and Helen took them for a while. Then I started attending with the boys but without Thomas. How did Thomas begin to go? When my father was dying, we took turns caring for him. The weekends were the only times I could go to Sacramento, so Thomas took the boys to church, and we all started going together! God is good. All the time.

Later Thomas and I were at a church service over the hill, and as they preached I began to cry. Frankly, I do not even remember what they were saying. I believe it was something about Jesus and His sacrifice for us, for me. They were encouraging anyone who had never truly accepted Jesus to come forward, now. How might I describe the feeling I had sitting in that seat way in the back of that church? I sat there and cried and cried. It felt like some sort of force was pushing me out of my seat and pulling me forward, up to the altar. I felt I just *had* to go. There was no way I could do otherwise. I wanted to shout it out to the world: I believe! I love Jesus! He is my Savior! I am His! Forever! I wept all the way to the altar and stood weeping tears of joy, of gratitude, for this great, great gift. I believe faith is a gift, but I also believe it is a choice. Interestingly, at that same church service there was an acquaintance who was sitting nearby. After my "altar call" experience, I spoke with him and shared what I had felt—the force pushing me up and out of my seat. He told me that he felt the exact same thing, but he chose to stay seated. And to this day, I am so extremely glad I got up out of that seat. Jesus filled my heart with hope. He gave me such a sense of peace. That "sick empty feeling inside" was no longer there. I was filled to the brim with His love.

Some time later I was at a CFO[62] camp in southern California, and the theme of the camp was repentance. One morning the speaker gave a talk on forgiveness, and somehow it moved me greatly. As I walked out of the meeting, a deep, deep nagging grew within me. It was as if someone were trying to tell me something—God perhaps? I stopped in my steps, looked up, and frantically asked out loud, "What? What is it?" Later in our prayer group, the leader reminded us of the theme of the camp, repentance. She suggested that each of us share anything we were wanting to repent of. That same deep nagging came bursting out, and I began crying out, "I'm sorry Lord! I'm sorry Lord, I'm so sorry!" The more I declared this the more I cried, and the freer I felt. I blurted out that I had never been baptized, and through all those tears I told our small group that I had to be baptized. Someone suggested that later we could go down to the lake and I could be baptized there. "No!" I cried, "No, I need to be baptized NOW." Another person looked around and pointed out that the young man in our group was a youth pastor, and he might be able to do it. "Yes!" I cried, "Yes!" But there was no body of water nearby, and by this point I was weeping and begging to be baptized. The young man grabbed his water bottle, which was sitting on the ground beside him. He quickly opened it up and poured it right over my head, and he baptized me in the name of the Father, of the Son, and of the Holy Spirit. As the water poured over me, I felt an incredible wave pour over and through me, with that same force I had felt pulling me out of my chair on the Sunday morning of my altar call. It flowed from my head through my entire body down to my feet. I was cleansed. I was forgiven. I was set free. Thank you, Heavenly Father! Thank you, Jesus! Thank you, Holy Spirit!

---

62 Camps Farthest Out. See https://cfonorthamerica.org/

This is the gift God has given me—a gift of faith—no matter the circumstances, no matter the hurt, I know that He is there. He has been there all along. The gratitude I have for this gift of faith is wide and deep, just like His love, as described in one of my favorite hymns:

> Oh the deep, deep love of Jesus,
> Vast, unmeasured, boundless, free!
> Rolling as a mighty ocean
> In its fullness over me,
> Underneath me, all around me,
> Is the current of Thy love;
> Leading onward, leading homeward
> To my glorious rest above.[63]

And the last lines from the film *La Vita E` Bella*: "Questa e` la mia storia." This is my story. "Questo e` il sacrificio che mio padre mi ha fatto." This is the sacrifice my Father has made for me. "Questo e` stato il suo regalo per me." This was His gift to me.

And I am forever grateful for His gift.

---

63 Text by Samuel Trevor Francis. The traditional tune by Thomas J. Williams can be found in many hymn books.

A Brief and Incomplete Description of My Spiritual Journey

Tom Mohamed

"Each of us is all the sums he has not counted," writes Thomas Wolfe in his autobiographical novel, *Look Homeward Angel*. Indeed, how do we understand ourselves and how we came to think, act, and believe as we do? Who am I? How did all this come to be?

My first introduction to faith happened when, as a small child, I knelt on a towel next to my Muslim grandfather, Sherrif Mohamed, as he prayed toward Mecca. I remember him as a kind man who faithfully prayed every day. At the time, we were living with my grandparents in Michigan City, Indiana, where I was born. It was a mixed Lebanese community of Orthodox Christians and Muslims living side by side. My great grandfather, Hussein Boudeeb Mohamed, was the founder of the first mosque in Michigan City.

My mother and father, Alta Clark and Hider Mohamed, divorced when I was four or five, and my mother moved us to Bonny Doon to be with her parents, Donna Mae Clark and Willard Clark. Mother worked as a librarian at the Fort Baker and Presidio libraries near the Golden Gate Bridge in San Francisco. She lived in the city with a friend and came home on weekends. Later my sister and I moved there to live with her.

When I was six or seven, the family of my best friend, Lewis, started taking me to church. Lewis was the son of Dr. Howie, the minister of Calvary Presbyterian Church in San Francisco. We would spend the whole morning there. Lewis's mom, Mrs. Howie, taught Sunday school and then took us to Dr. Howie's second sermon. Afterward she asked us questions about the sermon. It was all over my head, but Lewis and I enjoyed running around the church, and up and down several flights of stairs. (Calvary Presbyterian is huge!) In the summer, Lewis and I attended vacation Bible school. The baseball games were great! I received my first Bible from Calvary Presbyterian and even went Christmas caroling in San Francisco. I loved it all and of course learned some things about Jesus, but I understood very little. I was living amid domestic drama and trauma and mainly focused on my own personal survival and fulfillment.

Even though I did not absorb any theology at Calvary Presbyterian, I did develop a relationship with Jesus. We read about Him and sang about Him. I knew that He loved children and that He died sadly, but came back to life. And I learned that I should be good. I loved singing and I loved Christmas and Christmas carols. I loved buying gifts for my family: my mother, my grandparents, and my six sisters (two step, one full, three half). There is theology in Christmas carols, of course, and I loved them, but I didn't connect with them intellectually. By the time I was in high school, I had a very materialistic, secular view of life. Actually, I had no view at all. I was just trying to find my way.

All this changed one cold night when I was about 20. I was camping in the mountains with three friends. We were talking around the campfire when our conversation was interrupted by the need to put more wood on the fire. The dying of the fire caused us to begin talking about the fact that we would all eventually die, and that thought turned our hearts cold. We heaped on the wood. None of us believed that there was anything beyond this life, and I realized profoundly that I did not want to die. The coldness of that thought froze my heart, and it became clear to me that unless there was life beyond this life, anything I did was ultimately meaningless. Eventually everything would be lost and forgotten. When the sun turns into a red giant and destroys the Earth, all memory will be gone. The completely materialistic worldview I held at the time gave me *no hope*. One friend and I felt so cold in our hearts that we determined to talk until sun-up. That was 48 years ago.

I was despairing, and I wanted to know what was true, so when I returned to college at UC Berkeley, I changed my major to philosophy. I wanted to know: How did the universe come to be? Or had it always been? What was the Big Bang? And how could I begin to discover what is true? Philosophy didn't answer any of my deepest questions; however, the principles of logic I learned as a philosophy major are foundational for evaluating truth claims. The truth of a conclusion follows from the truth of the assumptions on which it is based. So philosophy did help me learn how to think.

At that time, there were many different spiritual groups and traditions on the Berkeley campus. It was the 1970's. The Hare Krishna groups were singing and chanting and handing out magazines. Holy Hubert Lindsey was debating all comers in Sproul Plaza. Ram Dass (born Richard Alpert) published the book *Be Here Now* about his spiritual journey from being a Harvard professor to finding a guru in India. Yogananda's 1946 book *The Autobiography of a Yogi* was also popular. Additionally there was the influence of the Beat poets and writers—Jack Kerouac, Gary Snyder, Lawrence Ferlinghetti—and their flirtations with Eastern thought and practices. I found all these things interesting, and as I delved into these different perspectives and practices, I was especially drawn to Yogananda and Ram Dass. For one, they believed in and spoke about a supernatural world and reincarnation. Reincarnation never made sense to me, but it asserted a non-material understanding of existence which, if true, gave me hope that my materialistic view of reality was false. The sincerity of these men gave me hope that I could believe their testimonies about their experiences. In a way it was my first experience of faith—in other words, believing in something I had never seen.

I found this time of spiritual searching very stimulating. I wanted to explore the differences and commonalities between Buddha, Confucius, Jesus, and Muhammad. One summer in Sacramento, I walked six miles to see *Jesus Christ Superstar* and then six miles back to where I lived, with my mind in a wonder. I did this two nights in a row. Ah, the balmy summer Sacramento nights! All my youthful experience in the Christian church had given me an affection and love for Jesus, but the gospel still didn't make sense to me.

At that time, I would guess that most people thought I was a nice and good person. I thought so myself, and this is not a joke. I rooted for the underdog, I loved animals, and I loved my family. All of us on some level have to justify ourselves to ourselves. This was my way. I was learning new ideas and had the sense that something was happening, that my life was just opening up. This was exhilarating, and yet, I still had a constant inner hunger and no sense of ultimate fulfillment or meaning.

It is an amazing thing then, that during the summer I had a profound inner experience which was transformative and felt like an awakening. I was at my house on a hot afternoon. I was sitting in a rocking chair and I was all tensed up inside. Then a thought came to me. I leaned back in the chair and relaxed, and somehow I let go inside. It was like a light came on inside of me and showed me . . . *myself.* That light, tied to my heartbeat, was an infilling of pure love, which somehow allowed me to see that I was selfish and self-centered in every aspect of my being. I was appalled by what I saw myself to be, and as detail upon detail of my vanity was shown to me, I rejected it. In my mind and heart I repented. I would not have used the word "repent" at the time, since that word was not part of my vocabulary, but that is what I did. I somehow *knew* that I needed to change. I also understood that it wasn't just me who had this problem. The whole world is broken. All too often, the energy (which I now understand to be the love of God) is only flowing inward, as light flows into a black hole, instead of flowing outward, which was happening to me during this experience. I remember thinking, 'Oh! so that is what sin is!' I had never understood the concept of sin, especially original sin, but I saw that it is a state of being, a profound inner selfishness, not a particular act. Sinful acts flow from the sinful heart.

The emptiness of the life I had been living was illuminated by this sudden infilling of light and love, and I knew from that experience that "higher consciousness" did exist. But it wasn't what I had expected. I wasn't going to develop a super brain that would intuitively know all things. What mattered was the heart and morality. The filled heart illuminates the mind.

This experience was essentially Christian, although not in any Christian setting. I discovered later that what I had experienced matched references in the gospels to the promise and working of the Holy Spirit. The experience that moved me to repentance was sacred and holy, and it convicted me. I began to tell my friends, "We need to change. We need to be pure. We need to be sincere." Something had happened to me!

I didn't know where to go with what I had experienced. One day while strolling through Sproul Plaza, I met some people from the Unification Church. They invited me to dinner and a lecture. The lecture was about building an ideal world, and the Unification Church, or "The Holy Spirit Association for the Unification of World Christianity," was the sponsor. The Unification Church believed that the Lord of the Second Advent had returned, and that now was the time to work for the coming of the Kingdom of Heaven on Earth.

I ended up joining the church and spent about three and a half years studying comparative theologies and working hard. We worked, sang, prayed, and studied, seven days a week, 16 to 20 hours a day. I spent most of my time on a mobile fundraising team. For a while I was the captain. There were about six to eight people on a team, and we did everything together. Each team had a territory, and we went from town to town within our territory. We covered the *entire* town, from early morning coffee shops, to day-time businesses, to night-time restaurants and bars, airports, parks, street corners—every location in that town. Work mostly involved selling flowers. After we had been everywhere, we moved to the next town. The remarkable thing is that although I was living a fairly cloistered life within our little fundraising team, I met and interacted with people from *every* walk of life and *all* different spiritual backgrounds. It was an eye-opening and profound experience. We were living outside of society, but we couldn't help observing the world, and we saw *everything*. This was the most challenging thing I have ever done.

Unification thought ran from creation in the Bible to present times, outlining the historical battle between God and Satan. Their studies compared different theories of history and its meaning. I was aware of my own ignorance and failings and was willing to submit to those I deemed knew more than me. I felt justified in following a leader as long as the leader did not ask me to commit a sin. I could follow, but I was responsible and would not blindly follow what *any* leader ordered me to do, if it was not Godly. At that time I learned how to pray. I developed my own relationship with God and Christ. If the Lord had called you 2,000 years ago, would you have followed? I felt called and I followed, but not blindly! I questioned everything and never lost the use of logic—questioning assumptions, questioning my own judgment. I wanted the world to be saved, but I never could really see the end goal of our movement. As I began to feel that I wasn't growing anymore and to sense that my family needed me, I left the church and returned home.

I was determined to live a Godly life. I don't claim to have done so! Our fallen nature is great within us! But I determined that instead of trying to save the world, which was beyond me, I would instead dedicate myself to my extended family and community. When I met my wife, Teresa, I shared with her my understanding of the holiness of the bond between husband and wife and the ideal of becoming spiritually one. I felt that my mission in life was to raise a God-centered family for the good of the world.

In 1987 Teresa and I moved to Bonny Doon. We were able to repurchase the property of my grandparents, Donna Mea and Willard Clark, which they had sold in 1977. This meant a great deal to me because I had spent so much time there as a boy. My grandmother sang in the Bonny Doon Church choir as I do now, and was one of the early members of the church. I can remember visiting Mr. and Mrs. Pyle, who lived in the Kirk House before the Presbyterian Church acquired the property. The church building itself was Mr. Pyle's workshop. Helen Robb, a longtime family friend, began taking our children to Sunday school, and then we began attending the church just as John Burke was installed as the new pastor. There we met the Murphy family, the Adamson family, and many others.

I have attended the Bonny Doon Church now for 30 years. I love Jesus and God and everything Holy. I cannot say exactly what will be. Christian theology is complicated when it comes to understanding the end times. The splintering of the Christian faith into hundreds of denominations seems tragic to me, as does the worldliness of so many denominations that has caused some churches to compromise with a corrupt culture. The early church martyrs did not seek such compromises.

I try to live by the light of the Holy Spirit. The birth, life, death, and resurrection of Jesus is the most profound story in existence, and this is what guides my life. The search for truth and meaning never ends. There is no ending to our understanding of God and His purposes. I believe that there is a great battle between good and evil in our hearts, in the world, and in the heavenly realms. I seek discernment and understanding from the Holy Spirit who is alive in the world. Jesus calls us through the voice of the Holy Spirit. We need to listen and obey.

Reflections:

On the inerrancy of scripture[64]—I find the wisdom and love expressed in the Bible to be the most profound of any book or literature or philosophy. However, I am of the opinion that "now we see through a glass, darkly," and only later will we see "face

---

64 The doctrine that the Bible is without error. See https://en.wikipedia.org/wiki/Biblical_inerrancy

to face."[65] If the Bible is the inerrant word of God, which I have no argument with, I still don't believe that fallen humans can understand it completely. Thus the divisions in the faith. It's almost a moot point, who or which group has the final say, especially about what will happen in the future. I love the scriptures, and in reading them I look for the movement of the Holy Spirit to guide me in my life.

As we come before God, all pretense and arrogant pride melt into repentance and humility. Faith becomes the honoring of the call of the Holy Spirit all the days of our lives.

The fear of the LORD is the beginning of wisdom: and the knowledge of the holy is understanding.

Proverbs 9:10 (King James Version)

So teach us to number our days, that we may apply our hearts unto wisdom.

Psalm 90:12 (KJV)

---

65 See 1 Corinthians 13:12 "For now we see through a glass, darkly; but then face to face: now I know in part; but then shall I know even as also I am known." (King James Version)

My heart is not proud, LORD,
    my eyes are not haughty;
I do not concern myself with great matters
    or things too wonderful for me.
But I have calmed and quieted myself,
    I am like a weaned child with its mother;
    like a weaned child I am content.

    Psalm 131:1-2 (New International Version)

But the Helper, the Holy Spirit, whom the
Father will send in My name, He will teach you
all things, and bring to your remembrance all
things that I said to you.
           John 14:26 (New King James Version)

    But wisdom is justified by all her children.
           Luke 7:36 (NKJV)

A Grandmother's Legacy

Sue Cannon

My first memory of coming to know God was while attending Sunday school with my Grandmother at the Church of the Brethren in Paradise, Butte County, California. I am not sure how old I was, but I remember learning simple stories and doing crafts. My folks moved to Nevada around the time I was in first grade, and we only visited my Grandmother now and then. When we moved back to Butte County, we began visiting Grandma's house every Sunday, often staying Saturday night and returning home once we'd had Sunday dinner after church. We did this for several years until we moved to Durham, which was farther away. At some point we only visited Grandma's house once a month or so. I began attending a small church within walking distance of our house and later helped watch children during the Sunday service.

During the summer of my freshman year of college at Chico State, I began attending the Church of Christ, and I was baptized there. I stopped attending church when I started my sophomore year, and I did not attend regularly again until my Grandmother became ill from cancer right after I turned 40. I had called out to God in prayer during difficult times, and my prayers had been answered, but I did not feel the desire to return to church. I will always remember the moment when I received the call to sort out my faith at a deeper level. I was listening to the radio as I drove from the Bay Area to Paradise to visit my Grandmother. I do not recall the exact words, but the message on the radio spoke directly to my heart and circumstances. Although I had a fulfilling career in high tech, a wonderful marriage, and great friends, I no longer felt that I could achieve the fulfillment I desired in life through my career, friends, or fun experiences. With my Grandmother no longer covering me in prayer, I now felt the need to take responsibility for my faith.

It was then that I began attending Bonny Doon Church. The first day I visited, Sherry McDermott invited me to join her Women's Bible Study. There I began studying the book of John and fully gave my life to Christ.

My Grandmother's church in Paradise, California.

The LORD is my shepherd; I shall not want.

He maketh me to lie down in green pastures: he leadeth me beside the still waters.

He restoreth my soul: he leadeth me in the paths of righteousness for his name's sake.

Yea, though I walk through the valley of the shadow of death, I will fear no evil: for thou art with me; thy rod and thy staff they comfort me.

Thou preparest a table before me in the presence of mine enemies: thou anointest my head with oil; my cup runneth over.

Surely goodness and mercy shall follow me all the days of my life: and I will dwell in the house of the LORD for ever.

Psalm 23 (King James Version)

Amazing Grace

by John Newton[66]

Amazing Grace! How sweet the sound
That saved a wretch like me!
I once was lost but now am found,
Was blind but now I see.

'Twas grace that taught my heart to fear,
And grace my fears relieved;
How precious did that grace appear
The hour I first believed.

The Lord has promised good to me,
His word my hope secures;
He will my shield and portion be
As long as life endures.

Through many dangers, toils and snares,
I have already come;
'Tis grace hath brought me safe thus far,
And grace will lead me home.

---

66 English clergyman and abolitionist (1725-1807). These words are in the public domain.

Led to Christ
by the Bonny Doon Church

Sara Osborn

My parents were raised Christian, but ours was not a Christian household. My only religion was the beautiful music that piped through the house on Sunday mornings—Connie Francis, Tennessee Ernie Ford, and others. I particularly liked the song "Rock of Ages."

My husband and I moved to Bonny Doon when our daughter Elizabeth was two. When she was five, she attended a summer class at Bonny Doon Elementary School, where she heard someone describe a program at the Bonny Doon Church. I took her to the church, and that is where our family was led to Christ.

When I was younger, I had been baptized so my older sister could get into a sorority, but I really had no idea what this meant. The Bonny Doon Church taught me. My husband Royce and I decided to let our children Beth and Peter make their own decisions about baptism. They both chose in their early teens to be baptized at the Bonny Doon Church. What a blessing!

"Over the Rainbow"[67] had always been my favorite song.

Somewhere over the rainbow way up high
There's a land that I heard of once in a lullaby
Somewhere over the rainbow skies are blue
And the dreams that you dare to dream really do come true.

. . . .

---

67 From the 1939 movie *The Wizard of Oz.*

After I gave my life to the Lord, I finally realized that God was the one I had been searching for. God's Kingdom was the place over the rainbow that I had been longing for, but I did not know it until then.

I learned to love Christian music and learned that I could sing. I made wonderful friends at the Bonny Doon Church who taught me so much. Marion Wahl, Sherry McDermott, and Ethelyn Robison (to name a few) helped me with my voice and reading music. I made many other friends at the church; some are lifetime friends—Teresa and Tom Mohamed and their boys, the Murphys, the Adamsons, the Burkes, Beatrice Easter, Patty Bianco, Mona Collins, Maryette Morris-Ladley—too many to list.

I feel closest to the Lord while singing. My brain shuts down and I just hear the Word. Singing is my worship time, at church, at home, and in the car. I might not know the Bible front to back, but I know Jesus, thanks to the Bonny Doon Church. Our family was blessed to be led to the Lord in Bonny Doon. While we were living there, we were protected from many catastrophes that could have taken our lives. God's amazing grace got us through serious illness, surgeries, family death, earthquakes, mudslides, collapsing roads, and much more.

Once, we held a sunrise service at the top of our property on Warren Drive for those hardy enough to hike up our hill. We could see Monterey Bay from there. We watched the sun come up while listening to soft music, and we spent some time in worship. Afterwards we fed everyone a hilltop breakfast of eggs, bacon, and sweets. Being able to share the beauty of that moment and worship with our church and friends was so special for our family.

After 18 wonderful years in Bonny Doon we made the hard decision to leave California. My husband Royce had worked for United Airlines for 25 years, but after 9/11, the airline went into bankruptcy. The county told us we could not split our five acres into two parcels because the coastal zone required five acres for a new parcel. Frank Murphy tried with his whole heart to get the two-and-a-half acres next to ours but did not succeed. In the end, the Lord led us to Minnesota, to a wonderful new church, to a home and schools where both Beth and Peter met their future Christian spouses. Later, my husband and I moved to a retirement community in Arizona. We attend a church nearby and continue to be blessed by God.

What a joy that our daughter Beth Osborn Campbell had the idea to make care packages for Bonny Doon after the CZU fire (see final chapter). Her idea exploded into a project, and both of our neighborhoods showed up with donations to help. Royce and I drove a U-Haul truck from Arizona to California to deliver these donations and bring some comfort to the mountain we will always call home—Bonny Doon Strong—where we became Christians, where we learned the meaning of community, and where we learned about physical and inner strength. "Bonny Doon My Country Home"[68] has more meaning now than ever before!

---

68 Song composed by Karen Elmore for the children of the Bonny Doon School, 1977. Listen to a performance by Andy Furman at https://www.reverbnation.com/AndyFuhrman/song/24044666-bonny-doon-my-country-home.

FRONT ELEVATION

**Frauke Zajac's drawing of the front of the church,
based on Sue Murphy's vision.**

A Vision that Sue Murphy
Received from God

On February 26, 2014, Sue Murphy experienced an extraordinary vision from God. She immediately shared this with the church and wrote down the following summary a few weeks later.

What I Experienced

In the early morning hours of February 26, 2014, I had an extraordinary experience that started just after midnight and continued to just after 5 a.m. I believe that this was a direct message from God. I have had experiences before of feeling very close to God physically, emotionally, and spiritually. This was entirely different.

I had gone to bed around midnight and was very tired. Just as I was drifting off to sleep, I had an image of a beautiful small stone church. For a time, it could have been minutes or much longer (I had no sense of time), I was in a "conversation." I was saying, "Oh, how pretty, I'll pass this idea on to someone in the morning; now I want to sleep." At some point I became very alert. I let go of sleep and entered the vision. I was seeing and feeling and knowing (hearing, but not really hearing). I cannot describe this experience well; I have never felt this way. I was in God's presence and power in some inexplicable sense.

The Vision

I saw a stone church building. It was so beautiful and yet unassuming. I felt power and at the same time a welcoming draw. It was very friendly. I went willingly to the door. There was a pitched roof with beautiful large timbers. This wooden part was a special shelter over the door. The door (I couldn't see the actual door) opened and I entered the sanctuary. It was breathtaking. The presence of God was palpable. It was dark yet light at the same time. I saw very large beautiful beams, wood on the steep ceiling, possibly wood on the walls. It was the Presence that I was most aware of. I did not walk in very far. I stood about 10 feet inside. I could not move in the vision or in my bed. I felt an amazing energy flowing through my body and yet not a muscle moved. I was held captive but did not want to be any other place. I was feeling God's power, and experiencing as much as I could handle. I stood in awe and wonder. It was not a foreign place. It was similar to our current building, but it was so much more, physically and spiritually. It was as if everything was magnified, sanctified, beautified. I did not walk around the room. I was not thinking. I was just experiencing the Presence.

This feeling of love within the building was also (again, I knew but without words) a promise of individual healing for each person, which would give each the power to more fully love others in God's divine grace.

Closer to the end of the experience, I saw an image of a mountain (but it looked like a mound of ice cream or a plum pudding with white sauce poured over it). It represented the love starting at the church and spreading over the community of Bonny Doon. There was great love and healing for the whole community. This outpouring of God's love was very integral to the whole experience.

Random Memories

The building was larger than what we have now, taller, wider, longer, but it was not huge. I had the sense that I was in the same place as the current building. It was holy ground. It was amazingly beautiful. The entrance was important. One step up to a roomy flat stone deck, covered by the pitched roof (this is a separate structure attached to the stone building). I was reminded of a vision Marge Roussopoulos had many years before, of Jesus standing in the sanctuary of our church.

My Response

Around 5 in the morning I was roused enough to realize I would never sleep unless I wrote about the experience. I went to the computer and wrote a letter to the people on our prayer list. I needed to share and to ask for prayer. I asked people to pray for confirmation that the vision was from God. I humbly thank everyone for praying.

Sue shared this vision with the church that morning and over the next couple of Sundays. At the time, Sue felt the vision indicated that we should build a new church building. She presented the vision to church members who were interested. Some thought we should move forward with a building. Others thought the vision was from God but there might be a different interpretation of what it meant. Sue felt that her job was to offer what she had seen to the church and let the congregation take it from there. A Saturday evening prayer meeting was started to pray about this and about other needs of the church. This bi-weekly prayer and potluck continues to this day, and is one of the blessings that has flowed out to our community from the vision.

Frauke Zajac made a beautiful architectural drawing using Sue's description and adding details to make a complete building, since Sue didn't see everything. This drawing now hangs on the wall of the Kirk House, and part of it is reproduced at the beginning of this story.

Several members of the Bonny Doon community volunteered their expertise. A new septic system was designed that would service the current building and support a new, larger building in the future. This system was then installed by community members. We are very grateful for our supportive Bonny Doon community. Thank you!

On June 26, 2019, Barbara Gaskell interviewed Sue about her experience.

Barbara: What stands out to you now that it has been five years since you were given this vision?

Sue: What I remember so clearly was lying in bed being immobilized—I couldn't move—but at the same time I was aware of all the blood flowing through my veins. There was just this amazing energy. This past year I read about a similar experience in a book being passed around the church [*The Grace Outpouring* by Roy Godwin and Dave Roberts, 2008].[69] I

---

69 In chapter 6, pages 116–118 of *The Grace Outpouring*, Roy Godwin describes the experience of one young man who went to seek God at the foot of a cross at the Ffald y Brenin Christian retreat center in Wales, only to find that he was unable to move or leave the spot near the cross for several hours. The next day he called his estranged wife and they both went to the cross where they received deep emotional healing for their lives and their marriage. Elsewhere in the book, Roy Godwin describes this experience as being, "Unable to move because of the weight of God's Glory" (page 124).

thought, 'Oh my God, that's what it was! This is not out of the realm of what God does!' I had never talked to anybody who had experienced anything like this.

Barbara: How did that make you feel?

Sue: It is so hard to come up with words. I was in this space, but it had a different feeling. There was light off to my right—coming through windows it seemed, a huge shaft of light. I knew that it was God, but it was light. I felt like I was on holy ground. When I was there it was just an incredible experience of *being*. It was timeless. I was standing in the presence of Jesus.

The History of

Bonny Doon Presbyterian

Church

Building the church.

[The following article was originally published in *Memories of the Mountain: Family Life in Bonny Doon 1800-2000,* written by the Ladies of Bonny Doon Club © 2004 and published by Author House. The article was originally called "The Presbyterian Church." It is reprinted here with the permission of the author. Photographs have been rearranged to fit the current format, and one of the original photographs was unobtainable.]

The History of Bonny Doon Presbyterian Church

Barbara Louv

Much of the information about this church's early history has been gleaned from the well-kept church albums of pictures and newspaper articles. Other information, more recent in its content, was taken from personal interviews.

In February of 1959, the Presbyterian Board of Missions sent Dr. George C. Westberg to survey the interests of the church in Bonny Doon. Dr. Westberg, a graduate of seminaries in St. Louis and Dallas, had retired after twenty-five years of full time ministry in various U.S. states. His wife, Irene, was also active in church school teaching and music.

Bonny Doon was growing. Dr. Westberg found a group of believers very eager to form the new church. They set up their first Sunday worship service on November 1, 1959, at the home of Harry L. McGivern located on Empire Grade, one-quarter mile south of the Ice Cream Grade intersection. The Westbergs traveled up from their home in Capitola every Sunday morning, and also on Tuesday evenings for a mid-week service. Twenty-seven adults and ten children made up the newly formed congregation.[70]

---

[70] The Harry McGiverns offered their home for services. Irene Westberg led the junior church and directed the music. The Duane Hodgkinsons played the piano and made highway signs. The Frank Winnifords made the lectern. The Henry Hanas were greeters along with the Angus Andersons. The main pianist was Mrs. Louis King. The Fred Colbuses continued to offer a place to worship when they bought the McGivern house. Mrs. Harold Harvey led the senior choir while Mrs. Wesley Hull was soloist and Mrs. Pat Helmer played the accordian. Others were the Merhas, the Richard Bairds, elders Albert Swain and Otto Thiesens.

The fledgling church needed to find a larger meeting place. "They investigated a two-acre piece of land near the airport on Empire Grade, but decided on another setting, 'Rattlesnake Hill,' as it was known to the locals then," according to Helen Robb. On May 1, 1960, four acres of the old Quistorf estate on Bonny Doon Road and Ocean Avenue, now Pine Flat Road, was bought by the San Jose Presbytery.

Mr. and Mrs. Max Pyle had rented the house on the new property before their move to town. Elderly Max had made all sorts of wooden toys and gadgets in a garage that had been turned into a workshop next to the four-room house, according to Donna Mae Clark. The workshop-garage would become the chapel or sanctuary of the church. The little house was to become a church school and meeting place. With many small and large improvements, it remains so today.

While the garage-workshop was being converted into a chapel with plans by architect Kermit Darrow and labor by the congregation of thirty, the worship services were conducted in the tiny house by Dr. Westberg starting on June 5, 1960.

On April 28, 1961, one and a half years after its start in a private home, the Bonny Doon Presbyterian Church went from a mission church to a full-fledged status with 38 charter members.[71]

In September 1961, Reverend James D. Otter replaced Dr. Westberg, who retired in August 1961. By this time various activities were in full swing: junior and senior choirs, high school groups, women's Bible studies, collections for needy

---

71 Amongst them were the Richard Andersons, Richard Bairds, Raymond Bensons, Louis Clarks, Ethel Davis, Allen Hall, Kenneth Hansens, Louis Kings, Louise Ludlow, Douglas Orwigs, William Pros, Alma Robinson, Shannon Sowerwine, Albert Swains, Alfred Welches, George Westbergs, and Frank Winnifords.

families, vacation Bible school, family night dinners, anniversary celebrations, picnics, and the hosting of meals for the chapel work groups.

During the early years, contributions from other churches included such things as chairs and silverware. In 1962, buying a coffeepot had to be put off by the ladies group for lack of funds. However, chapel building materials were purchased for $1,148. A new chapel roof was built for $388. The electric organ loaned by Allen Smith Organ Company was replaced in February 1964 with a new Wurlitzer spinet organ. The huge outdoor iron church bell was a gift from the Presbyterian church of Iron River, Michigan. It was set on a wooden tower and dedicated to the memory of Dr. George Westberg, who had died in early 1963. It continues to peal its welcome to worshipers even today.

A workday at the Presbyterian church.

In November 1961, the *Santa Cruz Sentinel* remarked on the congregation's work on the new church: "There's pioneering blood up among the oaks and pines and rolling hills of Bonny Doon. A rugged lot of worshipers are making a two-car garage and workshop seem a little more like a church."

Christmas Eve, Bonny Doon Presbyterian Church, 1968.

The Reverend James D. Otter, also a retired pastor, took the part-time leadership role from September 1961 until August 1964. He and his wife served the church three years. In 1962, he commented in an annual report, "Our church is now accepted in Bonny Doon as 'The Bonny Doon Church.' Many, who have no present relationship with our church, when speaking of it to me, say, 'Our Church.' This is a good sign and indication that we are building it into the life of the community."

The Reverend Robert A. Koenig was a student in a doctoral program when he served the church from October 1965 to June 1969, almost four years. Dick Wahl felt that his sermons were often quite analytical.

The Reverend Elwood Hunter reflected his love of God's natural creations in his children's sermons. "A seashell or a flower in the desert would demonstrate his point," according to Marion Wahl. He served the church from January 1970 to April 1973.

Dr. Joseph Gray with his wife Mildred came to be a part-time minister in July 1974, after leaving his beloved Navajo Indian church in Chinle, Arizona. I felt that his compassion and empathy for his fellowman developed a strong faith to share with us. He retired after seven years in October 1981, and now lives in southern California.

Reverend Jamie Watts was the part-time minister starting in April 1982. He was a homemaker dad for his young family while his wife worked in San Jose. Reflected in his sermons were his interests in social issues of the inner city. He died suddenly of a heart attack in June 1986, at the age of forty-six. A stained glass hanging of the Holy Spirit dove memorializes his service to the church people.

Reverend David Crawford came to the church in October 1986, and served the church for a year.

In November of 1987, Dr. Pard M. Keyser and wife, Kat, came to the church with "a very spirited, liberal approach," according to Marge Roussopoulos. He left in May 1989.

The first woman pastor, Reverend Marjorie Pearson, came in September 1989. Marjorie loved music and children's programs. She formed a community jug band and shared music at festive occasions. In September 1991, illness caused her to resign.

In April of 1992, Reverend John Burke, his wife Barbara, and three children answered the call to minister. John has served the Bonny Doon Presbyterian Church longer than any of its other ministers and continues to be its pastor today. [See addendum.]

As the number of young people increased, Ian Adamson and his wife Denby joined as assistant youth workers. Organists through the years have been Betty King, Corinne Gabriel, Marge D'Esposito, Katy Caldwell, and Ethelyn Robison.

During the later years, activities of the church increased. The congregation supplied dinners to needy neighbors, and the church allowed the use of the facilities by preschools and groups such as Alcoholics Anonymous. Their teenagers traveled to Mexico on work projects. Bible studies and telephone prayer chains served those in spiritual need. Christmas carolers sang to shut-ins.

The congregation contributed to both domestic and foreign missions and to the victims of local tragic happenings such as fire, mudslides, and earthquakes. Rummage sales and craft fairs raised money for future building expansion.

Slowly, the buildings have changed, although the original chapel and Kirk House still stand. Dick McDermott led many a work committee in the 1990's. A large window replaced the paneling at the front of the church. Dick explained to me, "Quite to my surprise, the old wooden cross fit perfectly into the new window space without human planning." Much electrical work to bring light into a dark chapel was donated by Ted Louv. Ernie Errat provided money for a chapel cupola and rooftop cross to be constructed. Dick built the framework of iron so that the cupola could be lifted by its cross by a Lonestar Cement Company crane to the roof of the church in one piece!

To beautify and endear the old Kirk House to its flock, Joan and Bob Neilsen, the Frank Murphy family, the Larry Kings, and a host of others added paint, paper, and curtains. The addition of a foldout snack bar by Bob Neilsen ensures a time of outdoor fellowship each Sunday after church. The warmth of reception to strangers and the relaxed worship service make this a very welcoming church in which to worship God and support fellow Bonny Dooners.

The present mission statement of the Bonny Doon Presbyterian Church is ". . . to worship and glorify God, bringing love, healing, growth and a sense of responsibility to each other, our neighbors, our world and our God. We have a mission to magnify Jesus, our Lord, to bring people into membership in His family, the Church, to train them to spiritual maturity, and equip them so they can accomplish their ministry in the community."

This history of the Bonny Doon Church (as reprinted above) was published in 2004. To bring it to the present time (2020), we (the editors) have written the following addendum.

In 2006, the Alpha[72] program was introduced to the Bonny Doon Church. This 11-week course, in which participants learn and discuss the basic truths of Christianity, was helpful to many. The church also ran a vacation Bible program for neighborhood children for a few years.

In January 2019, John Burke suffered a major heart attack and needed to retire to concentrate on regaining his health. He continues to be well loved by the members of the church. We are grateful for all the years of service he gave to us, to our

---

72 See www.alpha.org.

Lord, and to our community. An oral history of John and Barbara's time of service with the Bonny Doon Church follows this addendum.

In March 2019, Edd Breeden stepped in to take John's place as pastor of the church. We are delighted to have him among us, and grateful for his service and care. His personal story can be found earlier in this book.

In addition to our wonderful pastors, many people have made vital contributions to the church. Volunteers from both the church and the community enable the Higher Grounds coffee shop to operate every Thursday morning in the Kirk House, providing free coffee, food, and companionship to all who come. (Read more about it in "The History of Higher Grounds" near the end of this book.) Many older members of the community also come to the church every Thursday morning to pick up food bags provided by the Grey Bears (a nonprofit not connected with the church), and if the weather is nice, they often stay and chat.

David Borders built a small lending-library box that stands in the church parking lot. Available at all hours, it features a continuously changing collection of books. Improvements have also been made to the children's play area, which now features a swing set, playhouse, and sandbox. Evin Murphy built the playhouse as an Eagle Scout project with his Boy Scout Troop, and Elliot McDonough donated money for the project in memory of his wife. Liam Murphy built planter boxes around the church for his Eagle Scout project, and Connor Murphy redid the deck and painted the Kirk House. Bob and Dolores Hughes donated comfortable new chairs for the church. Georgia Randle donated the stove for the Kirk House kitchen. Dutch Schultz built a set of beautiful new doors for the church entrance. (See the photo on the back cover of this book.) These new, lovingly made doors bring more light into the back of the church, which is appreciated by all. More improvements continue to be planned, especially to the church kitchen and porch.

Bonny Doon Church provides bags of food a couple of times a year to Valley Churches United, a nonprofit that offers assistance to low-income residents in the area. The church also holds special events. In the past couple of years, these have included two evangelistic outreach events to the Bonny Doon community, organized and executed by Steve Stiles and John Burke, and two star-viewing evenings organized by Martin Gaskell. These were well attended and appreciated by many members of the greater Bonny Doon community.

Activities and services at the Bonny Doon Church have always been a collaborative effort. Up until early 2020, a typical week went like this: Carol Sedar led a women's Bible study on Monday afternoons. Martin Gaskell played the piano for Tuesday choir rehearsals and helped the group prepare a piece to sing the following Sunday. The Higher Grounds coffee shop (see next chapter) was open on Thursday mornings. During the Sunday service, Bob Hughes played hymns on the piano while the congregation sang. Ian and Denby Adamson and Aaron Mohamed led the children's music time, and Denby led the time of open prayer. All the small children together were in charge of collecting the morning offering. Several church members provided Sunday school for the children after the collection. Among them were Sue Murphy, Teresa Mohamed, Petra Schultz, Julia Mohamed, and until recently, Marion Wahl.

All that changed in late March 2020, when the COVID-19 pandemic gained a sufficient foothold in Santa Cruz County that everyone was required to stay at home and churches were closed. The Bonny Doon Church, along with many other churches in our area, switched to having online services. We are all grateful to Sue Cannon for helping get our online services up and running. At this writing, July 2020, Edd Breeden is preaching from his house. Similarly, Martin Gaskell plays the piano and Ian Adamson plays the guitar from their separate homes. Sue Cannon hand-delivered song and hymn books to many members of the church, so we can all join in with the music. The choir continues to meet online every Tuesday evening, and Martin Gaskell puts together recordings of their choral pieces to share with the church on Sunday. The Saturday evening prayer group also meets online. The Women's Bible Study recently began meeting in Carol Sedar's backyard, with everyone being very careful to "socially distance." It is an unusual time.

While we miss meeting together in person, and long for the day when we can reunite once again in our church building, this time has had some unexpected blessings. All of Edd's sermons can now be watched online, and some people regularly join our church services from as far away as Texas and Boston. We were blessed to have Selvan Xavier of Sahaara Charitable Society preach to us one Sunday all the way from India. It was a joy to pray together for our world from two different continents. Another silver lining: Frank Murphy has been overseeing an extensive remodel of the Kirk House kitchen, which is easier to do now that the building is not being used.

We do not know how much longer this pandemic will go on, but for as long as it lasts, we will continue to love and trust God, and we will do our best to cherish and support one another. May God bring all of us safely through this difficult time.

The Women's Bible Study

Carol Sedar

In 1968, a group of seven women first gathered to study the Bible and pray together. Many of those women have either passed away or moved from Bonny Doon, but the Women's Bible Study continues to meet once a week, 52 years later. Sharing our lives, both joys and challenges, along with an ever growing list of answered prayers, continues to deepen our faith. We are blessed with a rich fellowship as we learn how to apply scripture to our lives today.

The Women's Bible Study, 2020.
From top left to bottom right are Carol Sedar, Mary Rose Hellenthal, Cheryl Curry, Sue Oliver, Kathy Hardin, and Charlotte Milliner.

The Bonny Doon Church, 2020.

Inside the Bonny Doon Church, 2020.

The Kirk House, 2020.

Bonny Doon Church, street side, 2020.

The children's play area, 2020.

Interview with
John and Barbara Burke

B. Gaskell: Today is July 16, 2019, and I am at John and Barbara Burke's house in Scotts Valley, California. So let's start from the very beginning. I am curious, John—what made you decide to become a pastor?

John: Well, when I was in the service, I was a medic, and after I came out of the service, I went back to college and finished up with a pre-med degree. But in my junior year, I had a professor who said, "Would you like to become a doctor? I can get you into medical school in Canada if you want to go." I was praying about that, and I just felt like I should be thinking about ministry. It was more of a gradual thing. There wasn't any light-bulb moment; I was just thinking that maybe I should go to seminary and train to be a missionary. So I went off to seminary—not right away, but pretty soon after the summer was over. I worked in a hospital for a couple of months and realized this wasn't going to be for me. As soon as I got into seminary it was obvious that I had made the right choice. That was in 1975.

So after three years of seminary, I wasn't sure what I should do. I came home and talked with my Dad, who was a pastor. I was ordained, even though I didn't have a church yet. I looked at different churches, some in the Deep South, and then one became available in Friday Harbor, Washington, and that is where I went. They were looking for a youth pastor. I thought to myself, 'Well, you know, working as a youth pastor is a good way to start. I can work under someone and learn what I am supposed to be doing—get some direction and focus.' So I was up there for a year and a half, and we had a high school group and a junior high group. I was meeting with an elder, and we were praying almost every day for the island. One day we met a man, I can't remember his name right now, but he was interested in reaching men. So he hired a hall and put out some announcements, and pretty soon we had 40 to 45 guys coming. He brought in speakers, and some people were saved. That was the result of our prayers for the island. I started preaching once a month in the church, and they liked my preaching.

B. Gaskell: May I poke a bit deeper? You said that when you got to seminary it was obvious that you had made the right choice. Why?

John: Well, I think I had a sense of peace about it. I just felt settled once I got to seminary. Before I went there, I had been working in a hospital, and I was becoming depressed—feeling like I didn't know what I was doing. And then someone told me that I should be working in the psychiatric part of the hospital because I liked talking with people more than I liked doing the medical work. That was just a nurse's offhand comment, but it was interesting. I didn't make a strong church connection while I was working there, and I was getting very depressed. I needed to do something different, and going to seminary felt like the right thing to do.

I had been thinking for a while about maybe working [as a Bible translator] with Wycliffe,[73] so after seminary I did a summer with the Summer Institute of Linguistics [a Wycliffe partner organization] in North Dakota. That was where I discovered that I have a rather poor ear for language. They gave me a language, and asked me to develop a grammar and learn as much as I could about that language over a 10-week period. I

---

73 Wycliffe Bible Translators. See https://www.wycliffe.org.

learned a few things—you know—like, "What is your name?" and "My name is. . . ." The language was Hindi, which is really not that far from English. It is an Indo-European language. But I was not making good progress, so they met with me and said, "Well, we know you are theologically qualified, but in terms of being a linguist—you are not." So that was kind of devastating because that had been my dream for a long time. I mean—like many people, I believed in the hierarchy. You know—missionary first, then pastor, and then teacher, and then whatever. That was very traditional when I was growing up, so I thought I should be a missionary. But after that summer, I realized that I would probably not be a missionary. If you can't learn languages, you can't go and minister in a foreign country very well because you won't be able to communicate. So that was when I decided to try some ministerial work. I wanted a little sense of adventure, so I went off to an island. (laughter) I had never lived on an island before. It was exciting.

B. Gaskell: What has been your greatest joy in ministry? What has made your heart sing?

John: Well, I just have a general sense of joy about Christian work, but I think I have always known that I was a witness for Christ. I have had the chance to lead people to Christ, and that has been my greatest joy. It hasn't happened every year—I mean, some years several people have come to faith, and other years none. I have always felt that's what I am called to be—a witness. And it is an interesting thing because a lot of people who are pastors especially like the pastoral role. I enjoy talking with people, but if I am talking with someone, I am really thinking about whether they are Christian—not in the sense of judging, but more, "Okay, so is this person going to enter heaven, or are they not? And if they are not, what are we going to do about it?" Most recently I have been witnessing on the golf course. I have had some good conversations with people—you know, you join someone and pretty soon they ask who you are, and I say, "I am a pastor." I like to start conversations. This last year I bought a lot of Gospels of John, and I've been handing them to people and sometimes witnessing directly, or just giving them the gospel so they can read it for themselves. I've had a few refusals, but most people do not refuse the Gospel of John. The last year or so, especially since the heart attack, I have realized that I want to increase in love for all people indiscriminately, and that is a big thing for me.

[In an earlier interview, on June 1, 2019, we discussed the Burkes' long history with the Bonny Doon Presbyterian Church.]

B. Gaskell: When did you first hear about the Bonny Doon Church?

John: I first heard about the church about 27 years ago. A pastor or two had come and gone, and I heard that there might be a vacancy. I was pretty busy and initially I didn't feel like it was the right time for us to come up, but then Dick Dosker asked me if I would be interested, and I said I would pray about it. (Dick had been filling in at the Bonny Doon Church for some time while they didn't have a pastor.) We came up for a couple of Sundays around Christmas, and it went well.

Barbara: John wanted to get back into ministry, and it was a United Presbyterian church, which we thought would be a good fit for us.

John: Then we were interviewed by the Avakians (Ruth and Sparky). He was on the session [the governing body of the church], and they were in their 70's at the time. They interviewed us over dinner, down at the Davenport Inn. By that time I was actively seeking the church job, and they were considering several people. We successfully passed the interview, so I started, I believe on Palm Sunday. The next week, of course, was Easter. I was a little nervous to be a new pastor starting right on Palm Sunday. We started the sunrise service at 6:30 a.m. on Easter that year. My Dad had done the same thing at Felton Presbyterian Church, back in the 50's. We had about eight or nine people at that first sunrise service. So that was how our ministry began.

Barbara: The first Sunday after Easter, there were fewer than 10 people in the church, and we were five of them. It was really small. Our children were about four, seven, and nine years old, and they couldn't sit through the service. I was the only person there with children, so I had to stand up and take them out. I took them over to the Kirk House, and I sat with them and played a little bit, but inside I was thinking to myself, 'I can't do this. I will *never* be in church again. I'm going to be the Sunday school teacher for my own three children. We could just as well have Sunday school at home!' (laughter) That was so disheartening for me. I was not excited about this scenario at all.

B. Gaskell: Oh dear.

Barbara: But I love this story! It was either the next Sunday or the Sunday right after that, that Petra walked in. She lived in Bonny Doon. Now, Petra and I have another history. We met in a supermarket. We had children the same age who were sitting in the grocery carts, so like young mothers do, we started talking to each other. We had two Peters, my Peter and her Peter. Petra was the easiest person to love right away, so we became friends completely apart from Bonny Doon. We ran into each other a few other times, and we always recognized each other because of the kids.

So, she walked in. I didn't even know that she lived in Bonny Doon, and she brought her two little boys. Now there were five kids. I took the five kids out, and I was thinking, 'Okay, so we are beginning something here.' But again it was going to be me, right? Well, it wasn't more than one or two Sundays later that Sherry McDermott came. People started coming. If I remember correctly, just about every Sunday another person showed up. News was getting around that there was a new pastor and he had *children*. Between Petra, Sherry, and I, there were three of us, and we became the Sunday school. The three of us rotated. We didn't have any curriculum. We were teaching the Bible and telling stories, doing art projects and singing songs. That was Sunday school, and it went on for a while like that until the church grew.

John: It was interesting because the people who came had children. So all of a sudden there were 15 to 20 kids. Within a year we were able to start a regular Sunday school with regular teachers and all that. Barbara organized it. We went from zero to three classes. It was a miracle.

B. Gaskell: How else did you see the church change over the years?

John: Well, we all got older. (laughter) We went from being in our 30's and 40's to late 50's and 60's and even 70's. I was there for more than a generation.

One thing that happened was that the Bieneckes came. (They had several kids also.) They were part of the church for three or four years. Before they left, they gave the church a gift to help fund a new church building and challenged the congregation to match it. That was the beginning of our church building fund.

So when we had quite a few people in church (40 or 50 on a Sunday), we expanded the building. First the left wall was moved back by 4 or 5 feet, and then the right wall. When we moved the right wall back we found a well in the ground. It was a hand-dug well that was about 6 feet deep and had no sides. It was just sand and earth and had a cover over it. We had to fill it in. [74]

Somewhere in there, Dick McDermott fashioned a steeple in his workshop, and the interesting thing about the steeple was that he put a metal frame inside, but it was a solid frame that he somehow welded to the cross that sticks up on top. So, when they wanted to put the steeple up, they just picked it up by the cross and placed it carefully on top of the church. That was how the church got its steeple.

We also remodeled the Kirk House. Frauke Zajac [who is a professional architect] gave us plans for that, and we took out a

---

74 There were two wells on the church property. One was this hand-dug well that is now filled in. The other, which is currently in use, was dug by John Lingemann.

couple of walls. We went down under the rug and there was a beautiful redwood floor.

About 23 years ago we started having the holiday faires. We started those right after Thanksgiving and they were a success. Then about three years ago we started the spring craft faire.

Barbara: We used to have rummage sales, remember that?

John: And we kept adding money to the building fund. I think it has been 10 years since Sue Cannon started the Higher Grounds coffee ministry, and supplied a lot of the equipment that is used for that. The Saturday fortnightly prayer meeting started about five years ago.

Barbara: It started right after Sue Murphy had her vision of a new church and made that public. She is the one who actually called for the first prayer meeting. And then you [John] kept it going.

B. Gaskell: What are some of your dreams and hopes for the church?

John: (thinking) What I would like to see in the church, one thing certainly, is that people's faith would be established; that they would know why they believe, not only know who Jesus is, but know why they believe that Jesus is Savior and Lord, and why they should follow Him. Also, the task of evangelism, in Bonny Doon and in the whole county. This has been on my heart for many, many years, maybe 40 years or longer.

What people have always said about the church is that it is very warm and loving, that people care about each other. We introduced open prayer in the service some years ago.[75] I wanted people to learn how to pray for each other.

Barbara: Ian and Denby Adamson helped with that. That was definitely a ministry of theirs besides the music. Denby has always had a strong prayer ministry and has encouraged people to pray. And the Saturday prayer group has been going really well.

B. Gaskell: You have expressed on several occasions that you feel like there will be a revival in Santa Cruz and that you have a longing for it.

Barbara: There are other pastors around here that feel the same way. I think that is the exciting part. Now that we are visiting other churches we are hearing, or sensing that from other pastors. Peter's church [Christian Life Center] is praying, for sure. Vintage Faith Church for the last two years has had a backdrop on their stage that shows a map of the county from Davenport all the way down to Prunedale, with the names of all the cities on it. To me, this is impressive because I am very visual. John has been praying for these cities by name for years, and here was the same vision.

John: I continue to pray for the cities of Santa Cruz County, and also Monterey County, as well as a lot of other places on the West Coast especially. And I think at some point you need to realize that you are going to have to continue praying, and maybe

---

75 This is a time when anyone in the congregation can pray for any need.

it will happen in your lifetime and maybe it won't. My favorite story is the story of the Welsh revival. There was a prominent pastor who proclaimed, "Revival is coming! Revival is coming very soon!" He died the next year, and revival came the year after that. (laughter) Obviously, the glory is the Lord's and He will answer our prayers when He will.

Many revivals have started when the Holy Spirit moves on people. That is the other thing that is very important—man doesn't start revivals. Man can be renewed and can even start renewal movements, and some are really profound. But God is the one who starts revivals. In a renewal, pastors and leaders lead it. In a revival, the laity become excited; they lead it and the pastors observe and are thankful. It's completely different qualitatively. It is very important to understand this distinction.

B. Gaskell: That is really interesting. I never thought about it that way before. Thank you so much for explaining this, and for sharing your memories and insights with all of us.

Welcoming Pastor John Burke.

Putting the new steeple on the church roof.

The church bell.

Susanville

#DoGoodFeelGood

@susanvilleup

Sign up to be notified of our mobile giving

application when it is released!

www.susanville.com

The History of
Higher Grounds

Larry Vilardo

[*The following article was originally published as a blog post dated June 21, 2018,*[76] *called "Higher Grounds History." It is reprinted here with the permission of the author, who was the transitional pastor of Trinity Presbyterian Church in Santa Cruz when he wrote this piece.*]

Recently, while enjoying an espresso at the Higher Grounds coffee shop, I engaged in a discussion with Sue Cannon, one of the founders. The name "Higher Grounds" comes from the lines of an old hymn:

"Lord, lift me up and let me stand,
By faith, on heaven's tableland;
A higher plane than I have found;
Lord, plant my feet on higher ground."[77]

The Higher Grounds coffee shop is literally "heaven's table." The coffee and food are free, fabulous, and served to all comers. Volunteers donate and prepare espresso drinks, and prepare an alluring breakfast buffet. Guests often drift outside to pick up a Grey Bears food bag.

Sue has a real passion for the people in Bonny Doon: "I feel that there needs to be a place for dialogue, for people to see each other face to face and converse." It would be a dream come true if there was a place where people could meet on common

---

76 http://bonnydoonchurch.blogspot.com/2018/06/

77 This is the chorus to the hymn "Higher Ground," which can be found in many hymn books. The text is by Johnson Oatman, Jr. (1856–1922) and is in the public domain.

ground and then because of their interactions move to higher ground.

There was such a dream, and there is such a place. It is the Higher Grounds coffee shop, which meets every Thursday from 8 a.m. to noon. It was founded by the Presbyterian church of Bonny Doon as an outreach to the surrounding community. It is pleasantly located in the Kirk House adjacent to the sanctuary at 7065 Bonny Doon Road. Free WiFi is always available. However, seldom if ever will you see anyone on an electronic device. Instead the place hums with multiple conversations that range from local to national topics. On any given day there are published authors, musicians, retired scientists, firemen and firewomen, people from other countries (even an exchange student), and locals from the Bonny Doon area. Morgan, the editor of the local monthly newsletter, the *Battle Mountain News*, can often be found holding court in this diverse group.

The motto here is "We filter coffee not people." When speaking of the dynamic atmosphere, Sue said, "It is actually difficult for some people because everyone is so immediately friendly." And friendly everyone is. There is real care and compassion shared among the regulars and visitors. This care is made concrete by the distribution of 60 Grey Bears food bags each Thursday at the site. There are also seasonal drives to help Valley Churches United,[78] and a donation receptacle for that cause is prominently placed.

Operating Higher Grounds has taken real faith on the part of the church and cooperation between church and community volunteers. Sue mentioned that, "Many in the community thought that this would not work because people moved to this

---

78 A volunteer-powered, donor-supported nonprofit agency providing assistance to low-income residents in need. https://vcum.org/

area to be left alone." The opposite has been true. People love interacting, and delight in the refreshing drinks and incredibly good food provided at Higher Grounds. Everything is free, supplied by donations and prepared by volunteers. As a result of the welcoming atmosphere and excellent food, Higher Grounds serves as a community gathering center, senior center, local watering hole, and town square all rolled into one.

The original proposal was crafted by church members Sue Cannon, Teresa Mohamed, and Frauke Zajac. In 2010 it was discussed by the session (the name for the local church board). Originally the proposal called for Higher Grounds to operate two days a week—Tuesday and Thursday mornings, only in the summer months—and serve limited coffee drinks. In order to accommodate the Grey Bears distribution, it is now open year-round on Thursday mornings.

In the year 2010 the church and the community were all feeling the depths of the great recession. The timing for a new endeavor could not have seemed worse, but Sue felt that it was the right time. Like most nonprofits, the church was down in finances. That's when Sue knew in her heart that the church needed to take a risk. "When a call comes, it is hard to describe," she said. "I felt that it needed to be done."

The road was not easy. Not only did the board of the Bonny Doon Church have to come to a consensus—which they did with unanimous approval of the proposal—but there were some hiccups along the way. Some people dreamed even bigger and wanted to serve espresso. Miraculously a Jura espresso machine was donated from a business in town. When that machine ran to the end of its usefulness, donations were used to buy the current machine, a Quick Mill Anita.

The use of an espresso machine made upgrading the electricity necessary. Dave Potratz, a local, volunteered. Dave's wife, Teri, currently runs the volunteer list for the kitchen. When Sue told me that, "People often volunteer for reasons mysterious or mystical," I turned to the cook on call for that day, Andrew Klofas, and asked him why he volunteered. He said, "Because SiSi (Song) did." When I asked why she did, he replied, "I have no idea." The humility and enthusiasm of the volunteers is amazing. Teri volunteered to manage the kitchen personnel list after she retired as a teacher. She was looking for something personally fulfilling that would help the local community. She told me that this was complicated, since she and her spouse Dave had planned to live part of the time in San Diego. She asked Sue for an opportunity, and Sue suggested the volunteer coordination role since some aspects of it could be accomplished remotely. Teri is still acting on that call today. She works with a dedicated and well-trained team of volunteers, which includes David Potratz, Jean Myer, Robin Colleen, Mary Ellen Cook, Beatrice Easter, Stephanie Jessen, Sisi Song, Andrew Klofas, Anisa Griffin, Kathleen Hughes, Judy Wylie, and Petra Schultz. Sue Murphy, Carol Sedar, and Sue Oliver do shopping, and Denby Adamson and Carol Sedar prepare savory dishes for the group.

In the beginning, the church provided the volunteers and supplies. As the outreach developed, community members began to volunteer. No one who comes to Higher Grounds is required to donate or volunteer, but all are welcome to do so. Everyone works together seamlessly, which is a testament to the church leadership and the community spirit. Some volunteers wear many hats. Frauke, a church board member who was on the original planning team, did most of the hosting for the initial six months and still works on the food teams. Using her architectural skills, she also coordinated the decorating and repairs needed, since the common area in the house had not been updated for years. Frauke worked on a shoestring budget, and with predominantly volunteer help she created a homey living room where any and all feel at ease. The carpet was torn up and a beautiful redwood floor was exposed, adding to the warmth and character of the setting. Some volunteers are not as visible as their accomplishments. Every week for six years, Rich Smith set out two highly visible handmade road signs ("heavy signs," Sue emphasized) to announce the location and opening of Higher Grounds.

Sue is understanding and appreciative of all who contribute. She emailed me a list of other volunteers who have given generously of themselves; for example, "Steve Homan, who has been a great ambassador to us. Every week he is generous to take out the trash. Also there were eight months or so when I resigned and Meggin Harmon ran the show on her own. Right after I resigned, I had a major bike accident that landed me in the Stanford trauma center for four days. If Meggin had not taken over Higher Grounds for that period, we probably would have closed it. The Lord works in mysterious ways. After I recovered, Meggin had some health concerns that required her to resign.

"Marion Wahl and Carol Sedar have both walked alongside me throughout the whole time. I praise God for all that they have been doing and their sweet prayers. Denby Adamson was my prayer partner when things were bumpy as well. There were times when we had a few threatening people here with mental illness. Ian Adamson came and intervened in those situations. He has a nonprofit residence for mentally ill people in San Mateo."

In our conversation, Sue summed up one of the important lessons to be learned here, "I have learned something about how the gospel works. We need to volunteer to do good works. It actually releases endorphins in our brains and keeps us healthy."

The dreams of Sue and the local church and community are not stagnant. When I met with Sue she spoke of the 12 homeless children in the area. She began to brainstorm about ways to address this. Immediately everyone chimed in and there was a meaningful discussion. One of Sue's proposals was to have a station that parallels the "leave a book, take a book" kiosks seen around the county. Only this would be a community "leave a canned food item, and take an item."

Bonny Dooners often say they live in "a little slice of heaven." In the middle of that slice is heaven's table! It seems that dreams can come true when people of faith and community members work together. Looking forward to the future with hope and inspiration is what our world needs right now.

The CZU Fire

On August 16, 2020, wild lightning storms started hundreds of fires across California, including the Warnella and Waddell fires in Santa Cruz County. Two days later, shifting winds caused the Warnella and Waddell fires to rapidly expand and join with several other fires farther north in San Mateo County. The resulting huge fire was called the CZU Lightning Complex. The entire community of Bonny Doon was evacuated on August 18 and 19. By the time the fire was finally contained and residents were allowed to return, the fire had consumed 86,509 acres and destroyed 925 homes.

Six of those homes belonged to families from the Bonny Doon Church, including several whose stories are in this book. The church building survived with only minor damage to the roof and a melted water-storage tank, even though the fire burned right up to the parking lot. A pod of firefighters used the church as a rendezvous place, and we were told that they slept in the sanctuary. We prayed for their welfare and safety every day.

There are so many stories that could be told about this fire, some are of hardship and pain, and others of heroism and amazing community resourcefulness and love. There were also some wonderful answered prayers. When the fire broke out this book was nearly finished. We (the editors) quickly realized that if we started collecting and adding fire stories to it, we would soon have to double its length. So we are going to stop here, and leave the fire stories for some time in the future.

We would like to end with a quote from one of Pastor Edd Breeden's sermons, given on September 13, 2020, shortly after he had been able to visit the church property for the first time after the fire.

"I was glad the other day when I was told I could go back to the church in Bonny Doon. I had heard the stories but had not yet seen it for myself. It was a special joy to see the property, with all the burnt trees around it, and the buildings with very few marks of the fire on them, and to feel the presence of Jesus that surrounds that place. To stand under the great tree in front of the Kirk House and know of the blessings of Jesus that have poured out of that place for so many years—the touched lives, the special anointings, the celebrations of life, the moments of fellowship, so many ways that Jesus has blessed so many people because of the ministry of the Bonny Doon Church. I was deeply touched."

Edd went on to say, "Pray for the Doon and its welfare in every way. Pray too for the places you went into exile, the people that welcomed you into their homes and lives. Seek what is best for your friends, your neighborhoods, and your families. And in their well being, you will find peace and prosperity. When good things come to others around you, good things will come your way as well."